I0662912

Best Easy Day Hikes
Oregon's North Coast

Help Us Keep This Guide Up to Date

Every effort has been made by the author and editors to make this guide as accurate and useful as possible. However, many things can change after a guide is published—trails are rerouted, regulations change, facilities come under new management, etc.

We would love to hear from you concerning your experiences with this guide and how you feel it could be improved and kept up to date. While we may not be able to respond to all comments and suggestions, we'll take them to heart and we'll also make certain to share them with the author. Please send your comments and suggestions to the following address:

> The Globe Pequot Press
> Reader Response/Editorial Department
> P.O. Box 480
> Guilford, CT 06437

Or you may e-mail us at:

> editorial@GlobePequot.com

Thanks for your input, and happy trails!

A FALCON GUIDE®

Best Easy Day Hikes Series

Best Easy Day Hikes Oregon's North Coast

Lizann Dunegan

FALCON®

GUILFORD, CONNECTICUT
HELENA, MONTANA

AN IMPRINT OF THE GLOBE PEQUOT PRESS

A **FALCON** GUILDE®

Falcon and FalconGuide are registered trademarks of The Globe Pequot Press.

Maps created by XNR Productions Inc. © The Globe Pequot Press
The author used MapTech software to produce some source maps.

ISSN 1547-3228
ISBN 0-7627-2573-7

Manufactured in the United States of America
First Edition/First Printing

Contents

The Hikes

Oregon's
North Coast

Pacific Ocean

WASHINGTON

Seaview
Astoria
Warrenton
Seaside

Tillamook

Lincoln City

Depoe Bay

Newport

Waldport

Yachats

Florence

St. Helens

Vancouver

Portland

Tigard

Newberg

Woodburn

Oregon City

Molalla

Silverton

Salem

Gates

Corvallis

Albany

Lebanon

Sweet Home

Junction City
Santa Clara

Eugene

Springfield

Reedsport

Elkton

Oakridge

OREGON

Coos Bay

Coquille

Roseburg

Bandon

Myrtle
Point

Myrtle Creek

Port Orford

N

Kilometers

Miles

Acknowledgments

Thanks to my trail hiking partners who helped me to research the trails in this book, including my canine trail partners, Levi and Sage, who always make my hiking trips more fun. Also thanks to Scott Adams and all the other folks at The Globe Pequot Press for their help and advice.

Introduction

This book contains twenty-three easy day hikes starting in
Fort Canby State Park in southwest Washington and continuing south to Yachats, Oregon. Many of the hikes in this
book are located in state parks or the vast 630,000-acre Siuslaw National Forest.

Long sandy beaches, dramatic headlands, and large bays
characterize Oregon's North Coast. Because of its proximity
to Oregon's three largest cities—Portland, Salem, and
Eugene—you can expect crowds on this part of the coast
during the summer months.

Weather

Expect and prepare for wet weather on Oregon's North
Coast. The North Coast has the highest rainfall in the entire
state, with an average rainfall of 80 to 100 inches; some areas
in the Coast Mountain Range receive up to 200 inches.
November through March is the wettest time of year,
although there are some dry periods during winter when
temperatures can reach the mid-60s. The driest weather on
Oregon's North Coast is generally July through mid-October,
with average temperatures in the low to mid-60s in summer
and occasional warm sunny days that reach into the mid-70s.
Rain, wind, drizzle, and fog are common weather patterns
on the coast, so bring waterproof shoes, wool socks, a good
rain jacket, gloves, a hat, and an extra set of dry clothes.

Beach Safety

Keep the following in mind when you are visiting beaches on Oregon's North Coast:

- Avoid hiking out to isolated rocks, tidepools, or beaches or around headlands during the incoming tide.
- Be aware of water-saturated logs that weigh several tons; they could roll on top of you and crush you.
- Don't wade out too far in the surf. Strong currents and waves can swiftly carry you offshore. In addition, the ocean temperatures are very cold and can quickly sap your strength.
- Watch out for sneaker waves that can knock you off exposed rocks, headlands, and jetties.
- Don't climb on steep cliffs or rocks. Assume that all cliff edges are unstable, and stay away from them.

Wilderness Restrictions and Regulations

Oregon State Parks and the USDA. Forest Service manage most of the public lands on Oregon's North Coast. Some national forest trails require a Northwest Forest Pass, which is $5.00 per day or $30.00 for an annual pass. For information on participating national forests and locations for purchasing a Northwest Forest Pass, call (800) 270–7504 or visit www.naturenw.org.

Many state parks on the Oregon Coast require a $3.00 day-use pass, or you can purchase a $30.00 annual pass by calling (800) 551–6949. All Washington state parks require a $5.00 day-use parking pass; call (360) 902–8844 for information.

Trail Contacts

Hike 1: Washington State Parks and Recreation Commission, 7150 Cleanwater Lane, P.O. Box 42650, Olympia, WA 98504; (360) 902–8844; www.parks.wa.gov.

Hike 2: Astoria/Warrenton Chamber of Commerce, 111 West Marine Drive, Astoria, OR 97103; (800) 875–6807.

Hikes 3, 4, 6, 7, 8, 9, 10, 12, 14, 16, 19, 20, 21, and 23: Oregon State Parks and Recreation, 1115 Commercial Street NE, Suite 1, Salem, OR 97301; (800) 551–6949; www.oregonstateparks.org.

Hike 5: Cannon Beach Chamber of Commerce and Information Center, Second and Spruce Streets, Cannon Beach, OR 97110; (503) 436–2623; www.cannonbeach.org.

Hikes 11 and 13: Siuslaw National Forest, Hebo Ranger District, 31525 Highway 22, Hebo, OR 97122; (503) 392–3961; www.fs.fed.us/r6/siuslaw.

Hike 15: Bureau of Land Management, 1717 Fabry Road SE, Salem, OR 97306; (541) 375–5646; www.or.blm.gov/salem/html/yaquina/index.htm.

Hike 17: Hatfield Marine Science Center, 2030 South Marine Science Drive, Newport, OR 97365; (541) 867–0271; www.hmsc.orst.edu/visitor.

Hike 18: Lincoln County Public Works, 880 Northeast Seventh Street, Newport, OR 97365; (541) 265–5747; www.co.lincoln.or.us/lcparks.

Hike 22: Cape Perpetua Interpretive Center, 2400 Highway 101, Yachats, OR 97498; (541) 547–3289; www.newportnet.com/capeperpetua.

Zero Impact

Many of the trails throughout Oregon's North Coast are heavily used in summer. Because of their popularity, we, as trail users and advocates, must be especially vigilant to make sure our passing leaves no lasting mark.

These trails can accommodate plenty of human travel if everyone treats them with respect. Just a few thoughtless, badly mannered, or uninformed visitors can ruin the trails for everyone who follows.

Three Falcon Zero-Impact Principles

- Leave with everything you brought.
- Leave no sign of your visit.
- Leave the landscape as you found it.

Most of us know better than to litter. It is unsightly, polluting, and potentially dangerous to wildlife. Be sure you leave nothing behind, regardless of how small it is. Pack out all your trash, including such biodegradable items as orange peels, which might attract area critters. Also consider picking up any trash that others have left behind.

Follow the main trail. Avoid cutting switchbacks and walking on vegetation beside the trail. Select durable surfaces such as rocks, logs, or sandy areas for resting spots.

Don't pick up rocks, shells, feathers, driftwood, or wildflowers as "souvenirs." Removing these items takes away from the next hiker's experience.

Avoid making loud noises that may disturb others. Remember, sound travels easily along ridges and through canyons.

Finally, abide by the golden rule of all hikers: If you pack it in, pack it out! Thousands of people coming behind you will be grateful for your courtesy.

Ranking the Hikes

Although the hikes in this book are relatively easy, some are longer and have more elevation change than others. Here's a list of the hikes in order of difficulty, from easiest to hardest.

17	Hatfield Marine Science Center Estuary Trail
6	Oswald West State Park—Short Sand Beach
5	Cannon Beach
9	Munson Creek Falls
23	Heceta Head Lighthouse
21	Yachats 804 Trail
19	South Beach State Park
18	Mike Miller Educational Trail
12	Kiwanda Beach to Porter Point
14	Devils Punchbowl State Natural Area
20	Seal Rock State Recreation Site
7	Cape Meares State Park
16	Yaquina Bay State Park and Lighthouse
3	Fort Stevens State Park
15	Yaquina Head Outstanding Natural Area
22	Cape Perpetua Trails
1	Fort Canby State Park
4	Ecola State Park to Indian Beach
10	Cape Kiwanda State Natural Area
11	Pheasant Creek Falls and Niagara Falls
13	Drift Creek Falls
2	Cathedral Tree to Astoria Column
8	Cape Lookout

Map Legend

═══⑤═══	Limited access highway
══⟨101⟩══	U.S. highway
─⟨18⟩─	State highway
─[55]─	Forest road
───────	Paved road
───────	Gravel road
= = = =	Unimproved road
- - - - - - -	Trail
▬▬▬▬▬	Featured route
•──•──•	Powerline
┼┼┼┼┼┼	Railroad grade
— – – —	Forest/park boundary
⋈	Bridge
▲	Campground
Ⓗ	Hospital
❶	Information
▭	Lodging
◲	Overlook/viewpoint
Ⓟ	Parking
▲	Peak
⚘	Picnic area
▪	Point of interest/other trailhead
⚎	Rest room
START ‖‖	Steps
🚶	Trailhead
∥	Waterfall

1 Fort Canby State Park

This fun route combines three short trails in Fort Canby State Park that take you through an old-growth Sitka spruce forest, along scenic rocky coastline, and to the Lewis and Clark Interpretive Center and the historic Cape Disappointment Lighthouse. There are many additional hiking opportunities available in the park, including a short loop trail leading to the North Head Lighthouse.

Distance: 4.5 miles (with other options).

Approximate hiking time: 1.5 to 2.5 hours.

Permits and fees: $5.00 day-use parking fee.

Canine compatibility: Leashed dogs permitted.

Maps: Maptech: Westport/Mount St. Helens/Mount Adams/Columbia River, Washington; USGS: Cape Disappointment, Washington.

Finding the trailhead: From U.S. Highway 101 in Astoria, exit north onto the bridge across the Columbia River, following signs to Ilwaco and Long Beach. At the end of the bridge, turn left onto US 101 toward Ilwaco and Long Beach. Go 11.5 miles north on US 101 to Ilwaco. In downtown Ilwaco, continue straight (left) toward Fort Canby State Park. Travel south on Fort Canby Road for 3.6 miles and turn left into a gravel parking area and trailhead signed for the Coastal Trail. *DeLorme: Washington Atlas & Gazetteer:* Page 58 B1.

The Hike

Just a short drive north of Astoria is 1,882-acre Fort Canby State Park, located on the scenic Long Beach Peninsula in southwest Washington. This state park boasts 7 miles of hiking

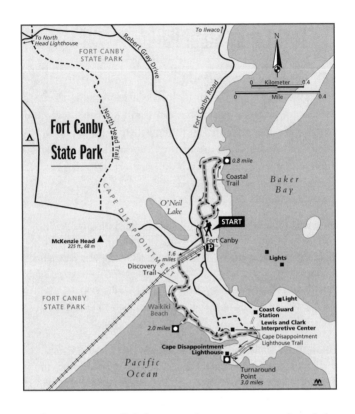

trails, two unique lighthouses, a large campground, and the Lewis and Clark Interpretive Center.

Start this route on the Coastal Trail, which loops through a large grove of old-growth Sitka spruce trees carpeted with abundant sword fern, blue-berried salal, and wood sorrel. After 0.8 mile you'll arrive at a viewpoint of Baker Bay. Here you can see Ilwaco to the north and a small wetland area filled with a variety of ducks and geese. After getting warmed up on the Coastal Trail, you'll walk up the campground entrance road to the start of the Discovery Trail. This trail starts by climbing a short hill to a secluded, rocky cove called Waikiki Beach and continues another 0.5 mile through a woodsy setting along a high bluff to the Lewis and Clark Interpretive Center. The interpretive center is open 10:00 A.M. to 5:00 P.M. daily and has a suggested donation of $2.00. The center has displays chronicling the journey of the Lewis and Clark Expedition, information on the building of the Cape Disappointment Lighthouse, and exhibits describing the maritime history of this area, which is known as the "Graveyard of the Pacific" due to the hundreds of ships that were lost attempting to cross the treacherous Columbia Bar (the mouth of the Columbia River). Large windows provide excellent views of the Cape Disappointment Lighthouse, the Pacific Ocean, and the Columbia River. After exploring the interpretive center, continue another 0.8 mile to a viewpoint of the Cape Disappointment Lighthouse. This impressive lighthouse, put into service on October 15, 1856, marks the entrance to the Columbia River. From here you'll retrace the same route back to the trailhead.

While you are visiting the park, be sure to visit the North Head Lighthouse. To get there from the Coastal trailhead, turn right and follow the paved park entrance road to the junction with Fort Canby Road (State Road 100). Turn left and continue to the junction with North Head Lighthouse Road. Turn left and continue 0.5 mile to the trailhead. Walk 0.3 mile to the impressive lightkeeper's houses and North Head Lighthouse, located on windblown North Head. The lightkeeper's houses are available for rent (360–642–3078). The North Head Lighthouse was built in 1898 as an additional navigation aid for ships entering the Columbia River from the north.

Miles and Directions

0.0 Start hiking on the signed Coastal Trail. Turn right at the next trail junction to begin the loop portion of the hike.

0.7 Turn right and walk down a side trail to a viewpoint of Baker Bay and a wetland area.

0.8 Arrive at the viewpoint. After enjoying the views turn around and head back to the main trail.

0.9 Turn right onto the main loop trail.

1.2 Go right where a sign indicates a return trail.

1.4 Turn right at the trail junction.

1.5 Arrive at the trailhead and the end of the Coastal Trail. To continue to the Discovery Trail, cross the park entrance road and walk along the paved campground entrance road.

1.6 Start hiking on the signed Discovery Trail, located on the left side of the campground entrance road.

1.7 Enjoy views of a secluded cove called Waikiki Beach.

2.0 Turn right and walk up a set of concrete stairs to a viewpoint of the Cape Disappointment Lighthouse and the Columbia River. After enjoying the views head back to the main trail and continue straight.

2.2 Arrive at the Lewis and Clark Interpretive Center. Turn right onto the paved path that circles the interpretive center, and watch for the signed Cape Disappointment Lighthouse Trail. Continue on the Cape Disappointment Lighthouse Trail to view the historic lighthouse.

2.5 Turn right at the trail junction.

2.7 Turn right onto a paved path that heads uphill toward the Cape Disappointment Lighthouse.

3.0 Arrive at the lighthouse. Retrace the same route back to the trailhead.

4.5 Arrive back at the trailhead.

2 Cathedral Tree to Astoria Column

This route explores a unique coastal forest right in the heart of Astoria. You'll get to view a 300-year-old Sitka spruce tree and climb to the top of the historic, 125-foot Astoria Column. From the top of the column, you'll have gorgeous views of downtown Astoria and the Columbia River.

Distance: 3.0 miles out and back.

Approximate hiking time: 1 to 1.5 hours.

Permits and fees: No fees or permits required.

Canine compatibility: Leashed dogs permitted; no dogs permitted in the Astoria Column.

Maps: Maptech: Newport/Portland/Mount Hood/The Dalles, Oregon; USGS: Astoria, Oregon.

Finding the trailhead: From U.S. Highway 101 in Astoria, turn south onto Sixteenth Street toward the Astoria Column. Travel 0.3 mile and turn left onto Irving Avenue. Continue 0.8 mile and park in a small gravel parking area on the right side of the road. *DeLorme: Oregon Atlas & Gazetteer:* Page 70 C3.

The Hike

As the oldest settlement west of the Rocky Mountains, Astoria is dotted with historical Victorian homes and has several museums dedicated to preserving its history. The town is named after John Jacob Astor, who helped establish Fort Astoria in 1811. The area began to grow when settlers, many of Scandinavian descent, arrived in the area in the 1840s. The town is located on the south side of the Columbia River not far from the Columbia Bar (the mouth of the Columbia River). This location was perfect for taking

Cathedral Tree to Astoria Column

Columbia River

To Seaside

Astoria

START

Irving Avenue

Cathedral Tree
0.3 mile

1.1 miles

Coxcomb Hill
595 ft., 181 m

Astoria Column

Turnaround Point
1.5 miles

Craig Creek

Youngs River

N

0   Kilometer   0.5

0   Mile   0.5

advantage of the huge salmon runs that existed on the Columbia River at that time. Salmon canneries, shipbuilding, and logging became the basis for Astoria's growth, and by the 1870s the community was the second-largest city in Oregon.

To learn more about Astoria's history, visit the Maritime Museum (1792 Marine Drive; 503–325–2323). This 37,000-square-foot facility celebrates the seafaring history of the Astoria area. The museum has seven galleries that include displays on the history of the salmon-packing industry, specifics on different types of boat design, and artifacts from the *Peter Iredale* shipwreck, which occurred near the mouth of the Columbia in 1906. This museum also has some modern maritime artifacts from the *New Carissa,* a wood-chip freighter that ran aground off Coos Bay in February 1999. The museum is open 9:30 A.M. to 5:00 P.M. daily.

You can get back to nature right in Astoria on this hiking tour, which leads you to an old-growth Sitka spruce called the Cathedral Tree and the historic Astoria Column. The hike begins on a wide gravel path that takes you through a mossy Sitka spruce and Douglas fir forest dotted with sword fern. After 0.7 mile you'll arrive at the 300-year-old Cathedral Tree, which is more than 200 feet high, 8.5 feet in diameter, and 27.5 feet around. The inside of the tree is hollowed out, making it appear as a natural cathedral. After viewing this grand old tree, you'll continue your tour with a moderate ascent for 0.8 mile to the Astoria Column, which is located atop Coxcomb Hill. This 125-foot-tall monument, completed in 1926, was built by the Great Northern Railroad and Vincent Astor (great-grandson of Jacob Astor). Climb to the top of the column on a steep, narrow 166-step spiral staircase. Once you reach the top, you'll have outstanding views of the mouth of the Columbia River where it meets the Pacific Ocean, Mount St. Helens, Youngs Bay, downtown Astoria, and the Astoria Bridge, which links Oregon and Washington. From here you'll retrace your route back to your starting point.

Miles and Directions

0.0 Start walking on a wide gravel path.

0.3 Turn right and begin walking on a wood ramp. Turn left at the next trail junction and continue a short distance to the Cathedral Tree. After viewing the tree go back to the last trail

3 Fort Stevens State Park

Shipwrecks, sandy beaches, and wetlands filled with wildlife await those who wander on trails and beachfront in Fort Stevens State Park. You can view the skeleton hull of the *Peter Iredale,* watch abundant bird life at the mouth of the Columbia, watch for migrating gray whales, take a stroll around scenic Coffenbury Lake, and learn about the area's history at the Military Museum located inside the park.

Distance: Varies depending on trails selected.

Approximate hiking time: Varies depending on trails selected.

Permits and fees: $3.00 day-use fee.

Canine compatibility: Dogs permitted.

Maps: Maptech: Newport/Portland/Mount Hood/The Dalles, Oregon; USGS: Warrenton, Oregon.

Finding the trailhead: To get to Fort Stevens State Park, travel about 4 miles south of Astoria (or 9 miles north of Seaside) on U.S. Highway 101; turn west and follow signs for 4.5 miles to the park. See the Miles and Directions section for detailed directions to different hiking opportunities in the park. *DeLorme: Oregon Atlas & Gazetteer:* Page 70 C2.

The Hike

Fort Stevens State Park encompasses 3,763 acres and offers a coastal habitat with a wonderful mix of shallow lakes, wetlands, coastal forest, and sandy beach, as well as a large campground. The park has an interesting history that dates from 1863, when the fort was established by President Lincoln during the Civil War in an effort to calm western military

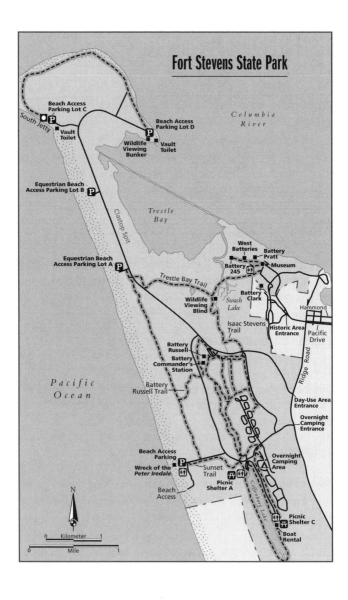

Fort Stevens State Park

Columbia River

South Jetty

Beach Access Parking Lot C

Vault Toilet

Beach Access Parking Lot D

Wildlife Viewing Bunker

Vault Toilet

Equestrian Beach Access Parking Lot B

Trestle Bay

Clatsop Spit

Equestrian Beach Access Parking Lot A

Trestle Bay Trail

West Batteries

Battery Pratt

Battery 245

Museum

Wildlife Viewing Blind

Swash Lake

Battery Clark

Isaac Stevens Trail

Hammond

Historic Area Entrance

Pacific Drive

Battery Russell

Battery Commander's Station

Battery Russell Trail

Ridge Road

Pacific Ocean

Day-Use Area Entrance

Overnight Camping Entrance

Beach Access Parking

Wreck of the *Peter Iredale*

Sunset Trail

Picnic Shelter A

Overnight Camping Area

Beach Access

N

Coffenbury Lake

Picnic Shelter C

Boat Rental

0   Kilometer   1

0   Mile   1

leaders' fears of increasing conflict with unionist states and territories. Luckily, the fort never saw military action. In the early 1900s Fort Stevens served as a strategic garrison to protect trade and transportation routes. During World War II, 2,500 soldiers stationed at Fort Stevens served under constant fear of attack from the Japanese navy. These fears were realized when a Japanese submarine approached the mouth of the Columbia River on the night of June 21, 1942, and fired on the fort. The seventeen fired shells did no damage, and no fire was returned because the submarine was out of range. Decommissioned after World War II, the fort was used by the reserves and the Coast Guard until 1975, when it was turned into a state park.

Today the park offers 5 miles of hiking trails, a large campground, and unlimited beach access. You can hike 2.4 miles around scenic Coffenbury Lake, which is popular for fishing, swimming, and boating.

If you want to see an old shipwreck, check out the *Peter Iredale.* In 1906 the four-masted British freighter was on its way from Australia to Astoria, Oregon, to pick up its next cargo. It was a very foggy, windy day, and as the ship approached the Columbia Bar, it became lost. Imagine the crew's frustration and fright when a strong gust of wind steered the ship aground onto Clatsop Spit. The crew survived, but the ship was so damaged that it had to be abandoned and left to fate. The rusty frame of this ship, buried deep in the sand, serves as a stark reminder of the brutal storms and merciless seas that have plagued sailors of both the past and present along this stretch of Pacific Coast. Also known as the "Graveyard of the Pacific" because of storms, rough seas, and fog, this area has caused more than 2,000 ships to wreck while trying to cross the Columbia Bar (the entrance to the Columbia River).

If you want to go whale watching, head to the viewing tower located in Parking Lot C at the north end of the park. Whales usually can be seen in December and March. Also be on the lookout for sea lions and harbor seals. This parking area also gives you access to miles of sandy beach. You can watch for abundant bird life by heading to Parking Lot D. A wood ramp leads you to a viewing platform overlooking Trestle Bay, which houses a productive estuary where you may see great blue herons, long-billed dowitchers, cormorants, and western grebes. From the same parking area, you can walk north along Clatsop Spit and watch ships crossing the Columbia Bar. Look for the trail on the north side of the parking area, and follow it for about 2.2 miles as it heads around the north end of Clatsop Spit to its ending point at the South Jetty.

You may also want to explore the abandoned gun batteries of the Fort Stevens Military Reservation, which guarded the mouth of the Columbia River from the Civil War until World War II. You can view military artifacts and interpretive displays at the Fort Stevens Military Museum (503–861–2000), located off Ridge Road adjacent to the park and open 10:00 A.M. to 6:00 P.M. June through September and from 10:00 A.M. to 4:00 P.M. the rest of the year.

Miles and Directions

To hike 2.4 miles around Coffenbury Lake, turn west at the campground entrance (the first park entrance) and go 0.2 mile to Picnic Area A at Coffenbury Lake.

To explore the wreck of the *Peter Iredale* as well as miles of sandy beach, turn left at the campground entrance (the first park entrance) and follow signs to a parking area near the shipwreck.

To watch for whales, sea lions, and bird life, head to Parking Area C. Turn west into the day-use Entrance (the second park entrance) and follow it to Parking Area C, on the left side of the road.

To walk around the tip of Clatsop Spit to view bird life and watch ships crossing the Columbia Bar, head to Parking Area D. Access the parking area by turning west into the day-use entrance (the second park entrance) and continuing to the road's end at Parking Area D.

4 Ecola State Park to Indian Beach

Located in scenic Ecola State Park, this classic coastal route offers a winding singletrack trail through a dense coastal forest with amazing ocean views and a picturesque beach for a finale.

Distance: 3.0 miles out and back.

Approximate hiking time: 1 to 1.5 hours.

Permits and fees: $3.00 day-use fee.

Canine compatibility: Leashed dogs permitted.

Maps: Maptech: Newport/Portland/Mount Hood/The Dalles, Oregon; USGS: Tillamook Head, Oregon.

Finding the trailhead: From U.S. Highway 101 at the north end of Cannon Beach, exit west at the ECOLA STATE PARK sign. Travel about 0.25 mile and turn right at a small sign for the park. Go 2.3 miles on a narrow, windy road to a large parking area and the trailhead. *DeLorme: Oregon Atlas & Gazetteer:* Page 64 A1.

The Hike

Ecola State Park covers 1,304 acres and displays breathtaking views from several viewpoints. For a warm-up be sure to head toward the ocean on a short paved trail that leads to expansive viewpoints looking south toward Cannon Beach and Haystack Rock. From this vantage point you may see the spouts of gray whales during their semiannual migration. These amazing marine mammals migrate south during December and January and return north in March and April. During Whale Watch Weeks—the last week in December

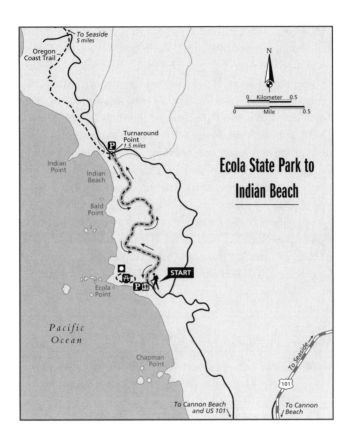

and the last week in March—trained volunteers can help you spot the whales.

This route begins on the north side of the main parking area and follows the Oregon Coast Trail north for 1.5 miles through mystical coastal forest of Sitka spruce and western hemlock to Indian Beach. Along the way you'll pass three spectacular viewpoints. Once you reach Indian Beach you can go beachcombing and watch surfers and boogie boarders catching waves offshore. From Indian Beach you'll have great views of the 62-foot-high Tillamook Rock Lighthouse that rests on a large chunk of basalt rock more than a mile offshore from Tillamook Head. This lighthouse, built in 1881, acted as a lifesaving beacon for ships headed for the Columbia River. Nicknamed Terrible Tilly, the lighthouse is now privately owned and does not allow public access.

From Indian Beach you have the option of continuing north on the Oregon Coast Trail for about another 6 miles as it weaves through coastal forest and travels over Tillamook Head to Seaside. To leave a shuttle vehicle at the northern trailhead in Seaside, travel about 10 miles north on US 101. In Seaside turn left (west) onto U Avenue; go 0.1 mile and turn left onto Edgewood Avenue. Continue for about 1.1 miles (Edgewood becomes Sunset Avenue) to the end of the road and the trailhead.

Miles and Directions

0.0 Look for a small trailhead sign on the north side of the parking lot. Pick up the singletrack trail as it winds through a dense forest.

1.5 Turn left at the fork that takes you to secluded Indian Beach (your turnaround point). From here, retrace the same route back to the starting point. **Option:** Continue 6 miles north on the Oregon Coast Trail to Seaside. Look for the trailhead on the right side of the Indian Beach day-use parking area.

3.0 Arrive back at the trailhead.

5 Cannon Beach

This beach trek starts in the quaint town of Cannon Beach and heads south on a spacious sandy beach where you'll pass 235-foot Haystack Rock. This distinct rock promontory is designated part of the Oregon Islands Wildlife Refuge and is an important nesting spot for several species of seabirds. At low tide you can explore the tidepools at the base of Haystack Rock and then continue your beach journey to the turn-around point at Tolovana Wayside.

Distance: 4.0 miles out and back.

Approximate hiking time: 1.5 to 2 hours.

Permits and fees: No fees or permits required.

Canine compatibility: Leashed dogs permitted.

Maps: Maptech: Newport/Portland/Mount Hood/The Dalles, Oregon; USGS: Tillamook Head, Oregon.

Finding the trailhead: Head about 73 miles west of Portland on U.S. Highway 26 to the intersection with U.S. Highway 101. Turn south onto US 101 and take the Cannon Beach exit. Continue driving south through downtown Cannon Beach to a public parking area located at the intersection of Second and Spruce Streets. *DeLorme: Oregon Atlas & Gazetteer:* Page 64 A1.

The Hike

The hamlet of Cannon Beach, located approximately 73 miles northwest of Portland, is a popular tourist destination and home to famous Haystack Rock. Tourists can stroll through the town's art galleries and boutiques, relax at its many cafes, and walk along the broad, sandy beach to view

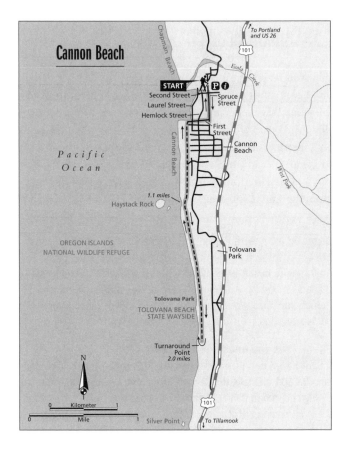

Cannon Beach

To Portland and US 26

101

Eola Creek

START

Second Street
Laurel Street
Hemlock Street

Spruce Street

First Street

Cannon Beach

West Fork

Chapman Beach

Cannon Beach

Pacific Ocean

1.1 miles
Haystack Rock

OREGON ISLANDS
NATIONAL WILDLIFE REFUGE

Tolovana Park

Tolovana Park
TOLOVANA BEACH
STATE WAYSIDE

Turnaround Point
2.0 miles

N

Kilometer
0   1

Mile
0   1

Silver Point

101

To Tillamook

235-foot Haystack Rock. The town is well-known for attracting artists and has more than a dozen art galleries that feature watercolors, oil paintings, ceramics, photography, fiber arts, bronze works, and blown glass. The town is also host to the annual Sandcastle Day (held in June), which features amazing sand sculptures by some of the best sandcastle builders on the West Coast.

Lewis and Clark traveled to the Cannon Beach area in January 1806 when Native Americans told them about a whale that had washed up on the beach. The whale was found at the mouth of a creek, which Clark named "Ecola," a local Native American term for whale.

Cannon Beach earned its name after a series of events that took place in the mid-1800s. In 1846 the U.S. survey schooner *Shark* sank near the mouth of the Columbia River. Within a month three cannons from the wreck washed up on the beach near Arch Cape, south of present-day Cannon Beach. The cannons later vanished, and legends developed regarding their disappearance. When Arch Cape built a post office in 1891, it was named Cannon Beach. As the area's population grew, four more post offices were built, three of which were designated Ecola. In 1922, residents voted to change the name of the post offices from Ecola to Cannon Beach, and the name has stayed ever since.

You'll enjoy this 4.0-mile out-and-back beach trek, which starts at the parking lot next to the Chamber of Commerce Information Center in downtown Cannon Beach. If you want to take along a lunch, stop at Osburn's Grocery Store and Delicatessen on Hemlock Street, just north of Second Street. Once you reach the beach, you'll turn south and arrive at 235-foot Haystack Rock after 1.1 miles. The origin of Haystack Rock began with a series of eruptions some seventeen million years ago that poured molten rock over the Columbia Plateau. The eruptions continued for more than ten million years, spreading lava over 78,000 square miles. Some of these lava flows reached the ocean, which was 25 miles inland from its present-day location. When the lava invaded the soft marine sediments of the coast, different knobs, sheets, and fingers of rock began to form. As the rock cooled, it turned into basalt. Over millions of years these basalt formations have eroded to form the rocky cliffs and headlands seen today along the coast of Oregon. Haystack Rock is one result of this erosion process. Part of the Oregon Islands Wildlife Refuge, Haystack Rock is an important nesting spot for puffins, pelagic cormorants, pigeon guillemots, and western gulls. At the base of Haystack Rock, you'll find tidepools filled with such colorful creatures as sea anemones, starfish, mussels, and hermit crabs. From Haystack Rock the route continues another 0.9 mile south to your turnaround point at Tolovana Wayside.

Miles and Directions

0.0 From the public parking area, turn left onto Spruce Street.

0.1 Turn right onto First Street.

0.2 Cross Hemlock Street and continue west toward the beach. Cross Laurel Street and then pick up the sandy path that takes you to the beach. Once you reach the beach, turn left (south) and enjoy a fun trek on the long, flat, sandy beach.

1.1 Pass Haystack Rock on your right. Check out the tidepools at the base of this rocky promontory.

2.0 Arrive at Tolovana Wayside (your turnaround point). Retrace the same route back to your starting point.

4.0 Arrive back at the public parking area and your starting point.

6 Oswald West State Park– Short Sand Beach

Take an amazing walk through a grove of old-growth coastal forest along the banks of Short Sand Creek to Short Sand Beach and Smugglers Cove in Oswald West State Park. Enjoy a day at the beach watching surfers and boogie boarders riding the waves, exploring tidepools, and enjoying gorgeous coastal scenery.

Distance: 1.0 mile out and back (with longer options).
Approximate hiking time: 1 hour.
Permits and fees: No fees or permits required.
Canine compatibility: Leashed dogs permitted.
Maps: Maptech: Newport/Portland/Mount Hood/The Dalles, Oregon; USGS: Arch Cape, Oregon.

Finding the trailhead: From the junction of U.S. Highways 26 and 101, turn south and travel 14.8 miles to a parking area on the left (east) side of the road in Oswald West State Park. *DeLorme: Oregon Atlas & Gazetteer:* Page 64 B1.

The Hike

Oswald West State Park covers 2,474 acres and encompasses some of the most beautiful landscapes on the Oregon Coast, including Neahkahnie Mountain, Arch Cape, Cape Falcon, Smugglers Cove, and Short Sand Beach. Named for Gov. Oswald West, in office from 1911 to 1915, the state park features many hiking trails and a walk-in campground. The sites

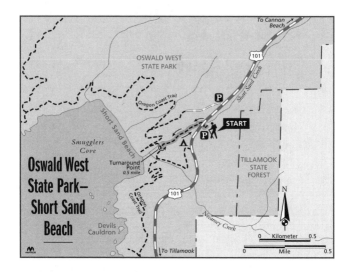

are first-come, first-served, and the campground fills up rapidly on summer weekends.

This route takes you on an amazing walk through a giant stand of old-growth Sitka spruce, red cedar, and Douglas fir trees along the banks of picturesque Short Sands Creek. Start your journey at the wood trailhead sign located on the north side of the parking lot. Walk on the paved path as it leads you under the highway and descends at a gradual pace next to Short Sand Creek. Most likely you'll share the trail with surfers and boogie boarders who are heading to Short Sand Beach and Smugglers Cove to spend the day riding waves.

Enjoy the soothing sounds of the creek and the lush greenery of huckleberry, salmonberry, and salal bushes that line the creek. Huckleberries have round red berries that are about 1 centimeter in diameter; salmonberries are shaped like a raspberry and can range in color from yellow to light reddish-pink; salal berries are bluish-purple, round-shaped, and grow in thick clusters. All three of these berries were an important food source for coastal Native American tribes. Salmonberries were mixed with fat and salmon to create a high-calorie food that was an important energy source during the harsh winter months. Native Americans also dried and mashed salal berries and huckleberries and made cakes out of them to be stored for later use. The leaves of the salal plant were applied to burns and cuts as a first-aid remedy. The leaves of the plant were brewed as a tea and used to treat coughs, heartburn, and tuberculosis.

After a short 0.5-mile walk next to the creek, you'll arrive at a picturesque picnic area shaded by towering Douglas firs. A short trail leads down a flight of steps from the picnic area to Short Sand Beach and Smugglers Cove, which is flanked by Point Illga to the south and Cape Falcon to the north. On summer weekends this beautiful beach is filled with sunbathers, surfers, boogie boarders, families, and dogs. If you are looking for a longer hike, you can head 2 miles north from the picnic area on the Oregon Coast Trail to Cape Falcon.

Miles and Directions

0.0   Start hiking on the signed paved path at the north end of the parking area. The path continues under the highway and then begins paralleling Short Sand Creek. Rest rooms and water are available at the trailhead.

0.1   Turn right where a sign indicates beach access. (The trail that goes right is signed for the campground.)

0.3   Turn right at the trail fork signed for beach access and the picnic area. Not long after this junction, you'll cross a footbridge over the creek. After crossing the bridge look for a

7 Cape Meares State Park

Cape Meares, located in Cape Meares State Park, is one of three scenic capes along the Three Capes Scenic Highway (the other two are Cape Lookout and Cape Kiwanda). A hike here includes numerous opportunities to view seabirds and migrating gray whales. Other attractions include the Cape Meares Lighthouse, which was built in 1890; old-growth Sitka spruce trees; spectacular ocean views; and abundant wildlife and coastal forestland. Plan on spending the better part of a day here—and be sure to bring your binoculars.

Distance: Varies depending on the trails selected.
Approximate hiking time: 30 minutes to 1 hour.
Permits and fees: No fees or permits required.

Canine compatibility: Leashed dogs permitted.
Maps: Maptech: Newport/Portland/Mount Hood/The Dalles, Oregon; USGS: Netarts, Oregon.

Finding the trailhead: From U.S. Highway 101 in Tillamook, follow the signs to Cape Lookout Loop Road (the Three Capes Scenic Highway). Drive approximately 10 miles west on the Three Capes Scenic Highway to the CAPE MEARES STATE PARK sign. To proceed to the main parking area, turn right (west) onto Park Road and drive 0.6 mile to a parking area.

From Pacific City, drive 26 miles north on Cape Lookout Road (the Three Capes Scenic Highway) to the CAPE MEARES STATE PARK sign. Turn left (west) and drive 0.6 mile on Park Road to the parking area.

To view the Big Spruce Tree, turn right into a pullout right before the Cape Meares State Park turnoff. A short loop trail will take you by the tree. *DeLorme: Oregon Atlas & Gazetteer:* Page 58 A1.

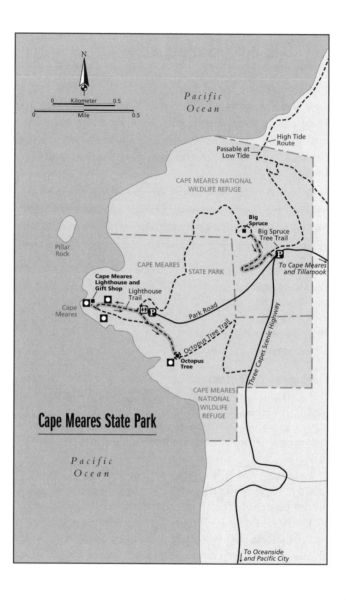

Pacific
Ocean

High Tide
Route

Passable at
Low Tide

CAPE MEARES NATIONAL
WILDLIFE REFUGE

Big
Spruce

Big Spruce
Tree Trail

Pillar
Rock

CAPE MEARES   STATE PARK

P

To Cape Meares
and Tillamook

Cape Meares
Lighthouse and
Gift Shop

Lighthouse
Trail

Park Road

Cape
Meares

P

Three Capes Scenic Highway

Octopus Tree Trail

Octopus
Tree

CAPE MEARES
NATIONAL
WILDLIFE
REFUGE

Cape Meares State Park

Pacific
Ocean

0   Kilometer   0.5

0   Mile   0.5

N

To Oceanside
and Pacific City

The Hike

The 233-acre Cape Meares State Park is a must-see stop for anyone traveling along Oregon's North Coast. This scenic cape is well-known for its large concentration of nesting seabirds and its historic lighthouse.

Start your exploration by walking down the paved 0.4-mile out-and-back Cape Meares Lighthouse Trail to the 40-foot-tall lighthouse. Along the way you'll pass seabird colonies nesting on the sheer 200-foot rocky cliffs. Bring binoculars for close-up views of these feathered cape residents, which include double-crested cormorants, Brandt's cormorants, pelagic cormorants, pigeon guillemots, common murres, and tufted puffins. Bald eagles and peregrine falcons also have been spotted in the area.

In 1886 the U.S. Army Corps of Engineers sent a representative to survey both the Cape Meares site and the Cape Lookout site, located south of Cape Meares, to see which would be more suitable for a lighthouse. After several days of surveying, the engineers picked the Cape Meares site because of its lower elevation, which would allow light to travel farther in foggy weather. Additionally, Cape Meares had a spring nearby that could provide fresh water and was more accessible than Cape Lookout. In 1887 Congress passed a bill that provided funding to begin construction on the lighthouse. A road was built to the site, and construction finally commenced in spring 1889. The interior walls were built with bricks made at the construction site, the exterior walls, from sheet iron shipped in from Portland. When the lighthouse was completed in November 1889, its light consisted of a five-wick oil lamp turned by a 200-pound lead weight.

Today's first-order Fresnel lens was shipped from Paris via Cape Horn and up the West Coast to Cape Meares. The lens has eight sides, four primary lenses, and four bull's-eye lenses covered with red panels. To view the intricate Fresnel lens, climb a series of steps to the top of the lighthouse tower. A gift shop in the lower section of the lighthouse is open daily May through September and on the weekends in March, April, and October.

If visiting the lighthouse isn't enough, check out the Octopus Tree. A 0.2-mile out-and-back, wheelchair-accessible trail leads from the main parking area to an ancient Sitka spruce whose low-slung branches truly resemble an octopus. The spruce was used as a burial tree by Native Americans; its octopus-like arms held canoes, where the bodies of the tribe's dead were placed. It is speculated that Native Americans bent the younger tree's more pliable branches outward into a horizontal position. Eventually the tree's branches continued to grow in the desired shape. The Octopus Tree is thought to have endured this ritual when it was very young, surviving to grow old and maintaining its odd shape.

To view another old-growth Sitka spruce, drive 0.6 mile to the park entrance and park in a dirt pullout on the north side of the road. A 0.4-mile out-and-back loop trail leads to a magnificent 400-year-old tree. As you walk the path, be on the lookout for odd-looking banana slugs. These interesting, slow-moving creatures eat plant matter and recycle the material back to the soil. They secrete a thin coat of mucus that helps them travel over the forest floor.

Miles and Directions

The Cape Meares Lighthouse Trail and the Octopus Tree Trail start from the main parking area. The Big Spruce Tree Trail begins at a dirt pullout on the north side of the park road just before the park entrance.

8 Cape Lookout

This route travels through a lush coastal forest of rare old-growth Sitka spruce to the end of scenic Cape Lookout in Cape Lookout State Park. Along the way there are magnificent views of Cape Meares to the north and Cape Kiwanda to the south. Gray whales can be seen in December, January, March, and April as they near the cape on their semiannual migrations.

Distance: 5.0 miles out and back.
Approximate hiking time: 2 to 3 hours.
Permits and fees: A $3.00 day-use pass is required. You can purchase a pass at the self-pay machine at Cape Lookout State Campground located north of the trailhead off the Three Capes Scenic Highway.
Canine compatibility: Leashed dogs permitted.
Maps: Maptech: Newport/Portland/Mount Hood/The Dalles, Oregon; USGS: Sand Lake, Oregon.

Finding the trailhead: From U.S. Highway 101 in Tillamook, head 15.5 miles southwest on the Three Capes Scenic Highway to the signed Cape Lookout trailhead on the right side of the highway.

From the intersection of Oregon Highway 18 and US 101 in Lincoln City, turn north onto US 101. Travel 14.6 miles north on US 101 and turn left (west) onto Brooten Road, where a sign states CAPE KIWANDA RECREATION AREA/PACIFIC CITY. Go 2.8 miles west on Brooten Road and then turn left onto Pacific Avenue toward Netarts/Oceanside. Continue 0.3 mile and then turn right onto Kiwanda Drive. Go 15.3 miles to the signed Cape Lookout trailhead on the left side of the highway. *DeLorme: Oregon Atlas & Gazetteer:* Page 58 B1.

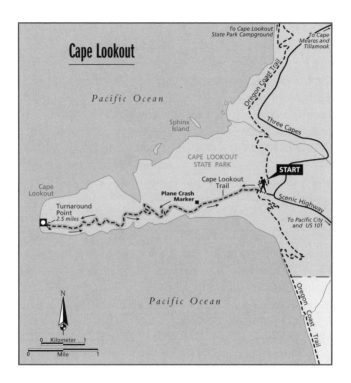

Cape Lookout

Pacific Ocean

Sphinx
Island

CAPE LOOKOUT
STATE PARK

To Cape Lookout
State Park Campground

To Cape
Meares and
Tillamook

Oregon Coast Trail

Three Capes

START

Cape Lookout
Trail

Scenic Highway

To Pacific City
and US 101

Cape
Lookout

Plane Crash
Marker

Turnaround
Point
2.5 miles

N

Pacific Ocean

Oregon Coast Trail

0   Kilometer   1

0   Mile   1

The Hike

Cape Lookout, part of 2,000-acre Cape Lookout State Park
(host to a campground, scenic Netarts Spit, and a variety of
plants and animals), is a spectacular headland made up of a
series of lava flows fifteen to twenty million years old. Jut-
ting into the ocean like an arrowhead, its 400-foot cliffs are
regularly pounded and carved by rhythmic waves and currents. The scenic cape is popular among whale watchers,
who come to observe gray whales during their semiannual

migrations—epic 10,000-mile round-trip journeys from breeding lagoons in Baja California, Mexico, to the rich Arctic Ocean and back again. The whales migrate south during December and January and north from March through April. Mature gray whales are 35 to 45 feet long and weigh anywhere from twenty-two to thirty-five tons. Females are larger than males and can live for fifty years—some males reach the ripe old age of sixty. The gentle giants feed on shrimplike amphipods by scraping mud from the ocean bottom and then filtering unwanted material through their baleen.

To reach the tip of the cape, take the trail that travels left just past the trailhead sign. The path begins by descending a series of switchbacks through a thick grove of Sitka spruce. These tough, stout trees are often referred to as "tideland spruce," and they thrive in the moist, cool temperatures that are characteristic of their coastal home. The Sitka spruce ranks with the Douglas fir and western red cedar as one of the largest tree species in the Northwest—only redwoods and sequoias are bigger.

Just over half a mile from the trailhead, the path arrives at a commemorative marker honoring an Air Force crew that perished nearby in a plane crash in August 1943. From here there are views of Cape Kiwanda and Cascade Head to the south.

Continuing on, the trail includes several convenient wooden boardwalks over the seemingly endless mire of mud. Up to 90 inches of rain falls annually along this stretch of the coast. The resulting foliage is striking—notice the bright green leaves of salal and salmonberry and the feathery fans of sword and maidenhair fern that cover the forest floor. After a while the trail reveals views of Netarts Bay,

Three Arch Rocks, and Cape Meares. The sandy, flat bottom of Netarts Bay makes it a perfect environment for such shell-fish as oysters, razor clams, butter clams, and crabs. The last half mile of the path is lined with Indian paintbrush, delicate wild iris, white yarrow, and bushy thimbleberry. The trail ends at a sharp point; if you look off the edge, you'll see the frothy Pacific pounding its huge swells against the rocky cliffs below. A convenient wooden bench has been placed at this classic viewpoint. Stay for a while and admire the view before heading back to the trailhead.

Miles and Directions

0.0 Start at the trailhead in the southwest corner of the Cape Lookout parking area. Take the trail that goes left. (The trail to the right heads north to Cape Lookout Campground.) Bear right at the first junction, just a few yards up the trail. (A left here will lead you along the Oregon Coast Trail to Sand Lake.) Descend through a thick grove of statuesque spruce trees.

0.5 Turn right at the trail fork.

0.6 A commemorative marker honors the crew of an Air Force plane that crashed 500 feet west of this site on August 1, 1943.

1.4 Enjoy a good view of the northern coastline and Cape Meares.

2.5 Arrive at the end of the official trail and your turnaround point. Retrace the same route back to the trailhead.

5.0 Arrive back at the trailhead.

⑨ Munson Creek Falls

Take an easy ramble among spectacular old-growth red cedar and Sitka spruce to a viewpoint of Munson Falls—Oregon's second-highest waterfall.

Distance: 0.6 mile out and back.
Approximate hiking time: 30 minutes to 1 hour.
Permits and fees: No fees or permits required.

Canine compatibility: Leashed dogs permitted.
Maps: Maptech: Newport/Portland/Mount Hood/The Dalles, Oregon; USGS: Beaver, Oregon.

Finding the trailhead: From the intersection of the Three Capes Scenic Highway and U.S. Highway 101 in Tillamook, travel 7.4 miles south on US 101 to the signed Munson Creek Falls State Natural Site turnoff on the left side of the road. Turn left (east) onto Munson Creek Road and go 1.5 miles to a circular parking lot and the trailhead. *DeLorme: Oregon Atlas & Gazetteer:* Page 58 A2.

The Hike

This short hike takes you along rambling Munson Creek, which is draped with big-leaf maple, old-growth western red cedar, and Sitka spruce. This small state natural site harbors what is thought to be one of the country's tallest remaining Sitka spruce trees, at 260 feet. As you hike the short path, enjoy the soothing sounds of the creek and look for edible salmonberries in midsummer. After 0.3 mile you'll arrive at a small picnic area and a viewpoint of the beautiful tiered cascade of 319-foot Munson Creek Falls—the highest in the Coast Range.

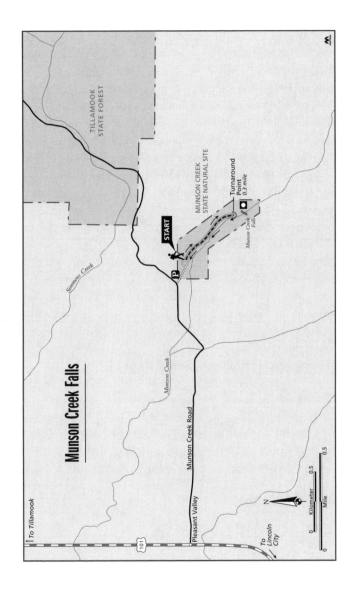

Munson Creek Falls

TILLAMOOK
STATE FOREST

MUNSON CREEK
STATE NATURAL SITE

START

Turnaround
Point
0.3 mile

Munson Creek
Falls

Simmons Creek

Munson Creek

Munson Creek Road

Pleasant Valley

↑ To Tillamook

101

To
Lincoln
City

N

Kilometer   0.5
0   0.5
0   Mile

Munson Creek Falls is not far from the friendly coastal city of Tillamook. The original inhabitants of the Tillamook area were three Native American tribes: the Nehalems, Nestuccas, and Tillamooks. These peoples were expert canoe builders and were often referred to as the "Canoe Indians." The first white settler in the Tillamook area was Joseph Champion, who arrived on the scene in 1851. Interestingly, he made his home in a giant spruce tree. During the next three years more settlers arrived in the Tillamook Valley. As a result of this growth, Tillamook County was established December 15, 1853, and Thomas Stillwell laid out the town of Tillamook in 1861. The growing community thrived on fishing, lumber, and dairy cattle.

The wet climate (more than 90 inches per year) and rich soils in the Tillamook Valley provide an excellent environment for raising dairy cattle. The valley is home to more than 150 dairy farms that raise more than 26,000 head of dairy cattle and produce in excess of $85 million worth of cheese and other dairy products per year. You can experience the cheese-making process firsthand at the Tillamook Cheese Factory Visitor Center, located 2 miles north of Tillamook on US 101. At the visitor center you can watch workers make cheese, view educational videos, and tour several interpretive displays. The cheese factory also has a cafe and gift store, where you can taste different cheeses, ice cream, and other tantalizing items. The visitor center is open daily, and admission is free.

Miles and Directions

0.0   Begin walking on the signed gravel path.

0.3   Arrive at a viewpoint of 319-foot Munson Creek Falls. Retrace the same route back to the trailhead.

0.6   Arrive back at the trailhead.

10 Cape Kiwanda State Natural Area

The route takes you on a beach trek and then to the top of Cape Kiwanda in Pacific City. You can explore tidepools, play in the surf, and enjoy spectacular views of Haystack Rock, Nestucca Bay to the south, and Cape Lookout to the north.

Distance: 1.0 mile out and back.
Approximate hiking time: 1 hour.
Permits and fees: No fees or permits required.

Canine compatibility: Leashed dogs permitted.
Maps: Maptech: Newport/Portland/Mount Hood/The Dalles, Oregon; USGS: Nestucca Bay, Oregon.

Finding the trailhead: From the intersection of Oregon Highway 18 and U.S. Highway 101 in Lincoln City, turn north onto US 101. Travel 14.6 miles north and turn left (west) onto Brooten Road where a sign states CAPE KIWANDA RECREATION AREA/PACIFIC CITY. Go 2.8 miles west and then turn left onto Pacific Avenue toward NETARTS/OCEANSIDE. Continue 0.3 mile and then turn right onto Kiwanda Drive. Go 1 mile and then turn left into the Cape Kiwanda public parking area adjacent to the Pelican Pub and Brewery Restaurant.

From Tillamook travel 25 miles south on US 101 and turn right (west) onto Brooten Road where a sign states CAPE KIWANDA RECREATION AREA/PACIFIC CITY. Go 2.8 miles west and then turn left onto Pacific Avenue toward NETARTS/OCEANSIDE. Continue 0.3 mile and then turn right onto Kiwanda Drive. Go 1 mile and then turn left into the Cape Kiwanda public parking area adjacent to the Pelican Pub and Brewery Restaurant. *DeLorme: Oregon Atlas & Gazetteer: Page 58 C1.*

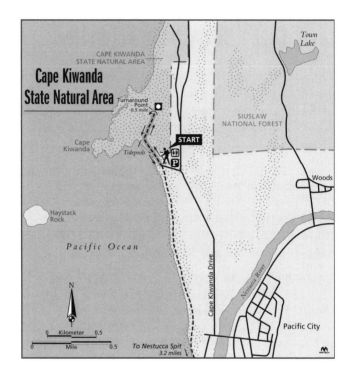

Cape Kiwanda State Natural Area

CAPE KIWANDA STATE NATURAL AREA

Turnaround Point
0.5 mile

Cape Kiwanda

Tidepools

START

SIUSLAW NATIONAL FOREST

Town Lake

Woods

Haystack Rock

Pacific Ocean

N

Cape Kiwanda Drive

Nestucca River

Pacific City

| 0 | Kilometer | 0.5 |
| 0 | Mile | 0.5 |

To Nestucca Spit
3.2 miles

The Hike

Pacific City, a coastal hamlet nestled next to the Nestucca River, is home to striking Cape Kiwanda—a golden sandstone headland sculptured by the relentless ocean swells of the Pacific. This small coastal town is well-known for its fleet of dory boats. Dories are flat-bottomed fishing boats, which can be launched off the flat sandy beach at the base of Cape Kiwanda. A local fleet still launches these boats into the calm morning surf to fish for halibut, lingcod, rock cod, and other commercial fish species that are plentiful around offshore Haystack Rock.

Local artifacts indicate that Pacific City (originally known as Ocean Park) began as a Native American village at the mouth of the Nestucca River. In the late 1800s white settlers moved into the area, developed the land for farming, and built a sawmill. Settlers also fished the rich Pacific waters. When a toll road was built from the Willamette Valley in 1880, visitors began traveling to this inviting coastal area. As the summer crowds began to swell, so did commerce. By 1895 the area hosted a campground, general store, and hotel. Visitors gained access to the beach via ferry, which was eventually replaced by much-needed bridges. In 1909 a post office was built and the name of the town officially became Pacific City. Not long afterward, a school was erected, and the area became a well-known resort destination.

You'll start this fun beach trek by heading north on Kiwanda Beach, where you can watch surfers and boogie boarders playing in the waves and anglers fishing offshore in dories. After 0.3 mile, stop to explore tidepools at the base of the dune, which is home to anemones, sea stars, mussels, and hermit crabs. After exploring the tidepools, you'll get a good workout on the steep and strenuous 0.2-mile ascent to the top of Cape Kiwanda. From the top you'll have spectacular views of Haystack Rock, Nestucca Bay to the south, and Cape Lookout to the north. For a longer beach adventure, you can head south from the parking area and hike 4.2 miles one-way to the end of Nestucca Spit. If you decide on this longer option, be sure to plan your hike at low tide.

Miles and Directions

0.0   From the parking area, turn right (north) and walk on the beach to the base of Cape Kiwanda sand dune. **Option:** Turn left and hike 4.2 miles one-way to the tip of Nestucca Spit.

0.3   Begin your 0.2-mile ascent of the Cape Kiwanda sand dune. Check out tidepools at the base of Cape Kiwanda.

0.5   Arrive at the top of Cape Kiwanda. Retrace the same route back to the parking area.

1.0   Arrive back at your starting point.

11 Pheasant Creek Falls and Niagara Falls

This easy forest trek leads you into a canyon to a viewpoint of Pheasant Creek Falls and Niagara Falls. Other pleasant trailside distractions include the opportunities to view black-tailed deer and elk, taste salmonberries and thimbleberries, and wade in bouldery Pheasant Creek.

Distance: 2.0 miles out and back.

Approximate hiking time: 1 hour.

Permits and fees: No fees or permits required.

Canine compatibility: Dogs permitted.

Maps: Maptech: Newport/Portland/Mount Hood/The Dalles, Oregon; USGS: Beaver, Oregon.

Finding the trailhead: From the intersection of the Three Capes Scenic Highway and U.S. Highway 101 in Tillamook, drive 15 miles south on US 101 (or 28 miles north of Lincoln City) to the small town of Beaver. Just past Milepost 80 turn left (east) toward the Nestucca Recreation Area and Blaine. Continue 6.7 miles to Blaine. In Blaine continue as the road veers right where a sign indicates to BIBLE CREEK ROAD. Go 5.1 miles and turn right toward Niagara Falls (this turn is easy to miss!). Travel 4.4 miles (the paved road becomes gravel after 0.3 mile) to an unsigned road junction. Turn right and continue 0.7 mile to a large gravel parking area. *DeLorme: Oregon Atlas & Gazetteer:* Page 58 A2.

The Hike

If you love waterfalls you'll enjoy this easy stroll to a viewpoint of Pheasant Creek Falls and Niagara Falls in the Siuslaw

Pheasant Creek Falls
and Niagara Falls

To US 101

SIUSLAW
NATIONAL FOREST

Mina Creek

Niagara Road

START

8533

Niagara Creek

0.8 mile

Pheasant
Creek Falls

Niagara Road

TILLAMOOK CO.
YAMHILL CO.

Turnaround
Point
1.0 mile

Pheasant Creek

N

Niagara
Falls

Niagara Point ▲
1,724 ft, 525 m

SIUSLAW
NATIONAL FOREST

0   Kilometer   0.4

0   Mile   0.4

National Forest. You'll begin by walking on a well-graded
forest path that descends through a second-growth forest of
Douglas fir and red alder carpeted with vine maple, sword
fern, and the delicate triangular springtime blooms of tril-
lium. Watch for elk or black-tailed deer darting across the
path or the loud calls of Steller's jays. Squirrels can also be
seen scurrying from branch to branch. Wood benches are
present at different intervals along the route, allowing you to
sit and enjoy the sights and sounds of the forest.

After 0.8 mile you'll cross a bridge and arrive at a view-point of the splashing cascade of 100-foot Pheasant Creek Falls. From this spot you can also see the feathery cascade of 130-foot Niagara Falls as it spills over a basalt ledge into a deep rock bowl. After another 0.2 mile you'll arrive at a picnic table and the trail's end next to picturesque Pheasant Creek. Look for edible yellow-colored salmonberries and red thimbleberries (a member of the raspberry family) that line the trail. The fruit of this plant is edible, and the leaves and flowers are high in vitamins and minerals and can be dried to make a wonderful-tasting tea. (Caution: This tea should be made only with completely fresh or dried leaves. During the wilting stage the leaves develop mildly toxic properties and should not be used.) Another fun distraction on this route is the opportunity to wade in the cool, bouldery creek.

Miles and Directions

0.0 Start hiking on Trail 1379, where a sign indicates 1 MILE TO NIAGARA FALLS TRAIL.

0.8 Enjoy views of Pheasant Creek Falls on the left.

1.0 Pass a picnic table on your left. Walk past the picnic table to a viewpoint of Niagara Falls at the trail's end next to the creek. After admiring the falls retrace the same route back to the trailhead.

2.0 Arrive back at the trailhead.

12 Kiwanda Beach to Porter Point

This beautiful beach trek heads north to the mouth of the Nestucca River. Beachcombing and wildlife watching are favorite activities on this route.

Distance: 1.8 miles out and back.

Approximate hiking time: 1 hour.

Permits and fees: No fees or permits required.

Canine compatibility: Leashed dogs permitted.

Maps: Maptech: Newport/Portland/Mount Hood/The Dalles, Oregon; USGS: Nestucca Bay, Oregon.

Finding the trailhead: From the junction of the Three Capes Scenic Highway and U.S. Highway 101 in Tillamook, travel south for 28.6 miles (or 14 miles north of Lincoln City) to the junction with Winema Road. Turn right (west) onto Winema Road and continue 0.6 mile to the road's end. *DeLorme: Oregon Atlas & Gazetteer:* Page 58 C1.

The Hike

This peaceful beach hike travels north on a long sandy beach to the mouth of the Nestucca River. Look for sand dollars and other seashells as you hike north. Sand dollars are close cousins to sea stars and sea urchins. They have a pancakelike body, thousands of tube feet, and velvety, densely packed spines and move through the sand picking up small, edible particles. When alive the animal can be colored gray, red, or purple.

Watch for brown pelicans flying above the waves, and listen to the loud calls of glaucous-winged gulls circling high

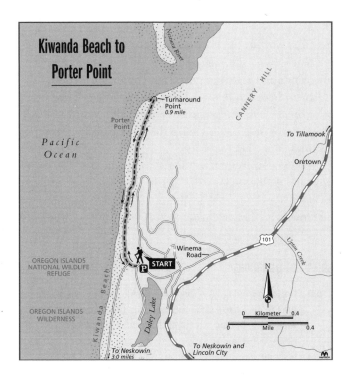

Kiwanda Beach to
Porter Point

- *Naskout River*
- Turnaround
  Point
  0.9 mile
- Porter
  Point
- *Pacific
  Ocean*
- CANNERY HILL
- To Tillamook
- Oretown
- 101
- *Upton Creek*
- Winema Road
- P START
- OREGON ISLANDS
  NATIONAL WILDLIFE
  REFUGE
- OREGON ISLANDS
  WILDERNESS
- *Kiwanda Beach*
- Daley Lake
- N
- 0   Kilometer   0.4
- 0   Mile   0.4
- To Neskowin
  3.0 miles
- To Neskowin and
  Lincoln City

above. You also may see western sandpipers running back and forth along the tide line, feeding on insects and small crustaceans. You can identify western sandpipers by their long black bill, reddish-colored head and shoulders, light-colored breast, and black legs.

After 0.4 mile you'll walk through a narrow opening between some large sandstone rocks that are covered with thousands of tiny barnacles. These tiny animals have a cone-shaped shell and are cemented permanently to the rocks. They filter plankton out of the water with a featherlike appendage.

As you continue, the beach becomes wilder and more mystical, with its frequent blanket of fog, salty ocean wind, crashing waves, and scattered piles of driftwood. After 0.9 mile you'll arrive at your turnaround point at the edge of the Nestucca River and Porter Point. Watch for sea lions swimming in the mouth of the river and resting on the sandy shore. From here you'll retrace the same path back to your starting point.

If you are interested in a longer hike, you can hike south from the trailhead along the beach for 3.3 miles to explore Proposal Rock, located in the small beach community of Neskowin. Neskowin Creek skirts the rock and offers plenty of fun wading opportunities.

Miles and Directions

0.0 Begin by walking on a short path that leads from the parking area to the beach. Once you reach the beach, turn right and walk north. **Option:** You can turn left (south) and walk 3.3 miles to Neskowin.

0.4 Walk through a narrow passage between a group of large sandstone rocks.

0.9 Arrive at the mouth of the Nestucca River and your turn-around point. Retrace the same route back to your starting point. Look for sea lions and harbor seals swimming in the river mouth and resting on the river's sandy shoreline.

1.8 Arrive back at the trailhead.

13 **Drift Creek Falls**

This forest path descends 340 feet, taking you on a fun tour through a thick coastal forest and across a magnificent suspension bridge over Drift Creek. From the bridge you'll have a grand view of the shimmering cascade of Drift Creek Falls.

Distance: 3.0 miles out and back.

Approximate hiking time: 1 to 1.5 hours.

Permits and fees: $5.00 Northwest Forest Pass.

Canine compatibility: Leashed dogs permitted.

Maps: Maptech: Newport/Portland/Mount Hood/The Dalles, Oregon; USGS: Devils Lake, Oregon.

Finding the trailhead: From U.S. Highway 101 just past Milepost 119 in Lincoln City, turn left (east) onto Drift Creek Road. Go 1.6 miles to the junction with South Drift Creek Road and turn right. Go 0.4 mile and turn left onto Drift Creek Camp Road. Continue 0.9 mile to another road junction signed DRIFT CREEK FALLS TRAIL and turn left. Continue about 9.8 miles (following signs to the Drift Creek Falls Trail) to a parking area on the right side of the road. *DeLorme: Oregon Atlas & Gazetteer:* Page 52 A1.

The Hike

You'll enjoy this popular forest trek, which begins by descending at a gentle pace on wide switchbacks through a second-growth Douglas fir forest carpeted with thick clusters of salal, sword fern, and edible salmonberries and bright-red huckleberries. You'll also be treated to a few remaining old-growth trees hiding deep in the canyon.

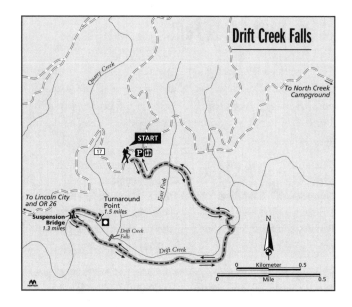

After 1.3 miles you'll arrive at the extravagant 240-foot-long expanse of the Drift Creek Suspension Bridge. Built in 1997 the bridge is anchored to a rock face on one side and bolted to concrete anchors on the other side. Bridge materials were flown in by helicopter, and the bridge span was assembled using a skyline cable rigging system that was suspended 100 feet from the canyon floor. The bridge is dedicated to trail builder Scott Paul, who died while working on the rigging for the bridge. From the bridge you'll have fantastic views of 75-foot-tall Drift Creek Falls as it plunges over a basalt ledge to the creek below.

After crossing the bridge you'll follow the trail another 0.2 mile as it descends to the edge of the creek. Wading in the creek during the hot summer months is a favorite activity. After cooling off in the creek, head back on the same route to your starting point.

Miles and Directions

0.0   Start walking on the signed trail that begins descending at a gentle pace from the parking area.

1.3   Cross a dramatic creek canyon on a high suspension bridge.

1.5   Arrive at the trail's end next to Drift Creek. Have fun wading in the creek and admiring the 75-foot cascade of Drift Creek Falls. Retrace the same route back to the trailhead.

3.0   Arrive back at the trailhead.

14 Devils Punchbowl State Natural Area

Churning waves, offshore rocks, and an interesting sea cave are some of the many highlights on this fun coast hike. This route begins with a tour of Devils Punchbowl, a collapsed sea cave, and then you'll take a stroll on Beverly Beach.

Distance: 2.8 miles out and back.

Approximate hiking time: 1 hour.

Fees and permits: No fees or permits required.

Canine compatibility: Leashed dogs permitted.

Maps: Maptech: Newport/Portland/Mount Hood/The Dalles, Oregon; USGS: Newport North, Oregon.

Finding the trailhead: From the junction of Oregon Highway 18 and U.S. Highway 101 in Lincoln City, travel south for 21.5 miles (or 8 miles north of Newport) and turn west at a sign for Devils Punchbowl. Go 0.2 mile to a T-junction and stop sign. Turn left and continue to the junction with First Street. Turn right and go 0.2 mile to the road's end at the Devils Punchbowl Day Use Area. *DeLorme: Oregon Atlas & Gazetteer:* Page 32, Inset 1, C1.

The Hike

This state natural area features dramatic rock formations and tidepools that can be explored at low tide. Begin by walking on the paved path that starts on the south side of the parking area next to the cliff's edge. When you look over the edge, you'll see waves frothing and churning in a collapsed sea cave that looks like a huge punch bowl. Wind, rain, and wave action have eroded the soft, sandstone rock that makes up this unique rock formation. From this cliffside viewpoint,

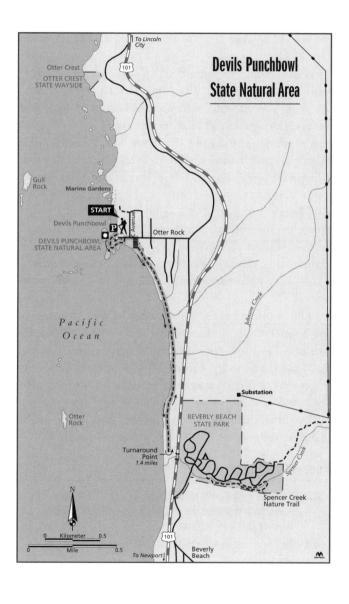

Devils Punchbowl
State Natural Area

To Lincoln City

Otter Crest
OTTER CREST
STATE WAYSIDE

101

Gull
Rock

Marine Gardens

START

Devils Punchbowl

DEVILS PUNCHBOWL
STATE NATURAL AREA

P

C Avenue

Otter Rock

*Pacific
Ocean*

Otter
Rock

Johnson Creek

Substation

BEVERLY BEACH
STATE PARK

Turnaround
Point
1.4 miles

Spencer Creek

Spencer Creek
Nature Trail

N

Kilometer   0.5
0

Mile   0.5
0

101

To Newport

Beverly
Beach

you'll also have nice views of a large offshore sea stack called Gull Rock.

Follow the paved path through a scenic picnic area sheltered by a thick grove of shore pine trees. The route continues along the sidewalk until you reach a set of stairs that descend through a small grove of Sitka spruce trees to Beverly Beach. Once you reach the beach, walk 1.2 miles south to the entrance tunnel to Beverly Beach State Park (your turnaround point). This large state park is one of the busiest on the Oregon Coast and features a large campground and a 0.75-mile nature trail that winds through coastal forest along the shores of Spencer Creek. (The trail can be accessed between Campsites C3 and C5.) In addition to regular camping sites, this park has yurts you can rent for the night, a large covered meeting hall, a visitor center, and a playground.

After returning to the parking area at Devils Punchbowl, you have the option of exploring rocky tidepools that are located a short distance north of the parking area. You can reach the tidepools by walking a few blocks up C Avenue and turning left onto an asphalt path that leads to the tidepools and a small, secluded beach. At low tide you can explore this abundant marine garden, filled with bright orange starfish, sea urchins, hermit crabs, and sculpin fish.

Miles and Directions

0.0 From the paved parking area, walk south on the fenced, paved path that hugs the cliff edge and provides dramatic views of Devils Punchbowl.

0.1 Turn right and walk on the paved path that parallels First Street.

0.2 Turn right and walk down a long set of wood stairs to Beverly Beach. At the bottom of the stairs, continue walking south on Beverly Beach.

1.4 Arrive at the entrance to Beverly Beach State Park Campground on the left (your turnaround point). Return on the same route back to the trailhead. **Option:** Turn left and go through the tunnel to Beverly Beach State Park Campground, where you can access the 0.75-mile Spencer Creek Nature Trail, located between Campsites C3 and C5.

2.8 Arrive back at the parking area.

15 Yaquina Head Outstanding Natural Area

The trails in the Yaquina Head Outstanding Natural Area take you through a rich coastal ecosystem, giving visitors an excellent opportunity to view seabirds, tidepool creatures, harbor seals, and migrating gray whales. The other main attraction of this special ocean oasis is the 93-foot Yaquina Head Lighthouse—the tallest lighthouse in Oregon. Bring a pair of binoculars in order to get a close-up view of the abundant wildlife this unique area has to offer.

Distance: Trails vary from 0.2 mile to 1.0 mile.
Approximate hiking time: 15 minutes to 1 hour, depending on the trails selected.
Permits and fees: $5.00 entrance fee, which is good for three consecutive days. You can also purchase an annual permit for $10.00.
Canine compatibility: Dogs are not permitted.
Maps: Maptech: Newport/Portland/Mount Hood/The Dalles, Oregon; USGS: Newport North, Oregon.

Finding the trailhead: From Newport drive 2 miles north on U.S. Highway 101. Turn left (west) onto Lighthouse Drive at the park sign. Drive 1 mile to the end of the road, where you'll reach a parking area. Be prepared to pay a $5.00 fee at the entrance station. *DeLorme: Oregon Atlas & Gazetteer:* Page 32 C1.

The Hike

Established in 1980, the Yaquina Head Outstanding Natural Area comprises one hundred acres of rocky basalt cliffs,

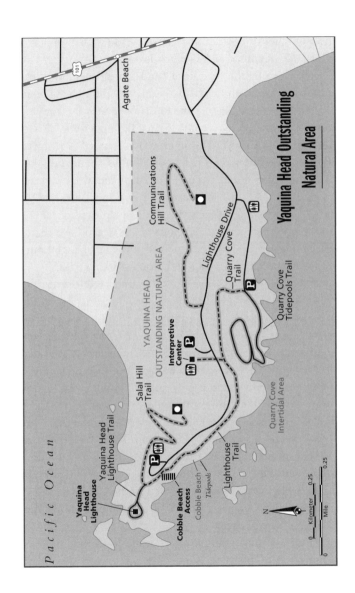

Pacific Ocean

Yaquina Head Lighthouse

Yaquina Head Lighthouse Trail

Cobble Beach Access

Cobble Beach Tidepools

Lighthouse Trail

Salal Hill Trail

YAQUINA HEAD
OUTSTANDING NATURAL AREA

Interpretive Center

Communications Hill Trail

Lighthouse Drive

Quarry Cove Trail

Quarry Cove Tidepools Trail

Quarry Cove Intertidal Area

Agate Beach

101

N

Kilometer 0.25

Mile

0

0

0.25

Yaquina Head Outstanding Natural Area

tidepools, rocky beaches, and grassy meadows that support a multitude of animal and aquatic life.

Managed by the Bureau of Land Management, this seaside oasis has many trails that lead you through different coastal life zones. Begin your tour of the area by stopping first at the interpretive center, located 0.7 mile from US 101 on Lighthouse Drive. The interpretive center has exhibits, video presentations, and hands-on displays about the geology and cultural and natural history of Yaquina Head. It's open 10:00 A.M. to 5:00 P.M. in summer and 10:00 A.M. to 4:00 P.M. in winter. Once you've filled up on facts at the interpretive center, turn right out of the interpretive center parking area and drive 0.3 mile to the end of Lighthouse Drive to the Yaquina Head Lighthouse Parking Area.

From the parking area take a leisurely walk over to the 93-foot-tall Yaquina Head Lighthouse. Construction on the classic seacoast tower began in fall 1871 and took two years to complete. Many of the building materials used for the lighthouse were shipped from San Francisco and unloaded in Newport. They were then brought out to Yaquina Head by wagon over a crude, rough road along the coast. It took more than 370,000 bricks to build the tower. A two-story building was also constructed next door to house the lighthouse keepers and their families. In 1872 a Fresnel lens arrived in sections from France; it was lit for the first time on August 20, 1873, by lighthouse keeper Fayette Crosby. In 1993 the lighthouse was refurbished by the Coast Guard and was officially designated a part of the Yaquina Head Outstanding Natural Area.

Tours of the lighthouse are available during summer from noon to 4:00 P.M. Winter hours may vary depending on the weather. From the viewpoint at the lighthouse, you may see gray whales during their winter migration, December through mid-February, or during their spring migration, March through May.

After touring the lighthouse take a walk down a long series of steps to Cobble Beach. This rocky beach and the offshore rocks and islands are all part of the Oregon Islands National Wildlife Refuge. While you're on the beach, keep your eyes peeled, because you may spot black oystercatchers, easily recognized by their dark black plumage, gold eyes, bright red bills, and pink legs and feet. These birds feed on chitons, limpets, snails, and other shellfish by picking the shellfish off the rocks with their long, sturdy beaks. In the rocky tidepools, you may see green anemones, prickly purple sea urchins, bright orange starfish, yellow sea lemons, oval-shelled mussels, volcano-shaped barnacles, turban snails, hermit crabs, and sculpin fish.

Looking toward the offshore islands you may spot some of the resident harbor seals. Your best chance at seeing harbor seal pups is during April and May. A glance toward the offshore cliffs and islands will reveal multitudes of seabirds, mainly Brandt's cormorants, pelagic cormorants, tufted puffins, common murres, and pigeon guillemots. During spring and summer, more than 24,000 birds nest on the cliffs and rocky islands surrounding Yaquina Head.

Back in your vehicle, drive 0.5 mile on Lighthouse Drive and turn right into the Quarry Cove Parking Area. The wheelchair-accessible Quarry Cove Tidepools Trail takes you on a tour of an area once quarried for the hard basalt rock used to build roads. Today the area has evolved into a thriving intertidal ecosystem.

Miles and Directions

The Quarry Cove Parking Area is located on the left side of the road 0.5 mile from the intersection of Lighthouse Drive and US 101. From this parking area you can access the Quarry Cove Trail, Communications Hill Trail, and the wheelchair-accessible Quarry Cove Tidepools Trail.

The interpretive center is located on the right side of the road 0.7 mile from the intersection of Lighthouse Drive and US 101. From this parking area you can access the Lighthouse Trail and the Quarry Cove Trail.

The Yaquina Head Lighthouse Parking Area is located 1 mile from the intersection of Lighthouse Drive and US 101. From this parking area you can access the paved trail to Yaquina Head Lighthouse, a stairway that takes you to Cobble Beach, and the Salal Hill Trail.

16 Yaquina Bay State Park and Lighthouse

This route explores the Yaquina Bay Lighthouse, built in 1871. After exploring the lighthouse you'll take a stroll on a long sandy beach to the historic Nye Beach District in Newport, which is host to the Newport Visual Arts Center and fun shops.

Distance: 2.9 miles out and back.

Approximate hiking time: 1.5 to 2 hours.

Permits and fees: No fees or permits required.

Canine compatibility: Leashed dogs permitted.

Maps: Maptech: Newport/Portland/Mount Hood/The Dalles, Oregon; USGS: Newport South, Oregon.

Finding the trailhead: From the junction of U.S. Highways 101 and 20, travel 1 mile south on US 101 and turn right (west) at the Yaquina Bay State Park sign. This turn is just before you cross the Yaquina Bay Bridge. Continue 0.2 mile to a parking area on the left side of the road. *DeLorme: Oregon Atlas & Gazetteer:* Page 32, Inset 1, C1.

The Hike

The Yaquina Bay State Recreation Area covers thirty-six acres and is located on the north side of Yaquina Bay in Newport. This popular and often-crowded park is filled with paved walking paths, picnic areas, and interpretive signs that describe the history of the area.

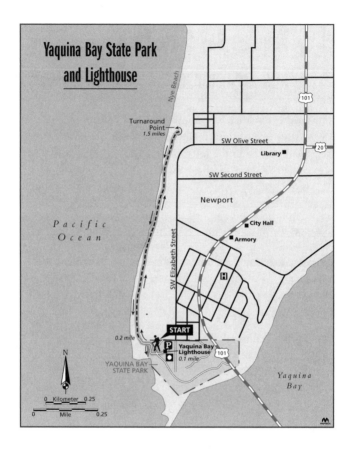

From the parking area walk across the paved entrance road and climb a series of steps to the 40-foot-tall Yaquina Bay Lighthouse, perched at a high point on a short bluff. Built in 1871 the lighthouse served as the entrance light to Yaquina Bay and is the last wooden lighthouse remaining in Oregon. Charles Pierce, the original lighthouse keeper, made a salary of $1,000 per year. Charles, his wife, and seven children lived in the house. Water was collected in a cistern and hand-pumped into the kitchen, and meals were cooked on a wood-burning stove. The lighthouse was decommissioned in 1874 when a new, brighter Yaquina Head Lighthouse was built 4 miles farther north in 1873. The decommissioned lighthouse fell into near ruin until the citizens of Newport and the Lincoln County Historical Society saved it from demolition in 1934. It has been fully restored, and you can tour the inside from 11:00 A.M. to 5:00 P.M. daily May through September and from noon to 4:30 P.M. October through April.

After checking out the lighthouse, cross the paved entrance road and head down a series of steps through a thick stand of shore pine and salal, through some small sand dunes, to a long sandy beach. Before you descend, soak in the views of Yaquina Bay and the historic Yaquina Bay Bridge.

Once you reach the beach, turn right (north) and walk on the beach for 1.3 miles to historic Nye Beach. As you hike this stretch of the route, keep your eye out for sandpipers and dunlins hunting for small crustaceans and worms along the shoreline and the far-off spouts of migrating gray whales (December through June). At Nye Creek you have the option of walking up a series of stairs and continuing to the Newport Visual Arts Center (777 Northwest Beach Drive). This center showcases the art of many Northwest artists in the 1,000-foot Runyan Gallery and the 300-square-foot Upstairs Gallery. The Runyan Gallery is open 11:00 A.M. to 6:00 P.M. Tuesday through Saturday; the Upstairs Gallery is open noon to 4:00 P.M. Tuesday through Saturday. After touring the galleries, take time to stroll through the many fun shops and restaurants of this historic district. From Nye Beach you'll retrace the same route back to your starting point.

Miles and Directions

0.0 From the parking area, cross the entrance road and read interpretive signs under a white-roofed building located on the right side of stairs leading to the lighthouse. After reading the interpretive signs, head up the stairs to view the lighthouse.

0.1 Arrive at the lighthouse. After you are finished with your tour, head back down the stairs and cross the entrance road to the day-use parking area and walk down a set of stairs to the beach. From the top of the stairs, you'll have great views of the Yaquina Bay Bridge, the north jetty, and Yaquina Bay.

0.2 Arrive at the beach and turn right (north).

1.5 Arrive at historic Nye Beach, where Nye Creek empties into the ocean (your turnaround point). Retrace the same route back to the trailhead. **Option:** Turn right and explore the Newport Visual Arts Center and the shops in the Historic Nye District.

2.9 Arrive back at the trailhead.

17 Hatfield Marine Science Center Estuary Trail

This short paved trail explores the 3,900-acre Yaquina Estuary, located on the south side of Yaquina Bay in Newport. The nature trail is adjacent to the Hatfield Marine Science Center, which has a variety of displays that give you a closer look at the plants and animals that live on the Oregon Coast. Be sure to explore the exhibits in the science center after you complete the hike.

Distance: 1.0 mile out and back.

Approximate hiking time: 30 minutes to 1 hour.

Permits and fees: No fees or permits required.

Canine compatibility: Dogs are not permitted.

Maps: Maptech: Newport/Portland/Mount Hood/The Dalles, Oregon; USGS: Newport South, Oregon.

Finding the trailhead: From the junction of U.S. Highways 101 and 20 in Newport, travel 1.8 miles south on US 101 to the sign for the Hatfield Marine Science Center. Turn onto OSU Drive and go 0.7 mile. Turn right at a sign for the Hatfield Marine Science Center Parking Area. Proceed 0.2 mile to the parking area. *DeLorme: Oregon Atlas & Gazetteer:* Page 32, Inset 1, C1.

The Hike

Begin the hike by walking on the paved path next to the water's edge. After 0.2 mile you'll arrive at a wood picnic shelter, where you can sit and observe a variety of birds—as well as stay dry if it's raining. Watch for blue herons hunting

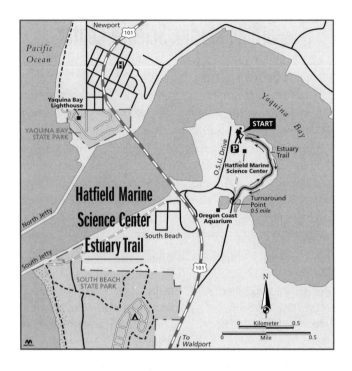

Map labels:
- Newport
- 101
- Pacific Ocean
- Yaquina Bay
- Yaquina Bay Lighthouse
- YAQUINA BAY STATE PARK
- START
- Estuary Trail
- O.S.U. Drive
- Hatfield Marine Science Center
- P
- Turnaround Point
  0.5 mile
- **Hatfield Marine Science Center Estuary Trail**
- North Jetty
- South Jetty
- Oregon Coast Aquarium
- South Beach
- SOUTH BEACH STATE PARK
- 101
- N
- Kilometer 0.5
  0   Mile   0.5
- To Waldport

for fish and small reptiles. Also be on the lookout for whimbrels using their long, probelike beaks to search for small crustaceans and worms along the muddy shoreline. Dunlins and sandpipers can also be seen probing the mudflats for food. Farther offshore you may see Brant's geese, which spend the winter in the estuary feeding on abundant bright-green eelgrass. These birds have a black head, neck, and breast; dark brown backs and undersides; and a white neck-band and tail feathers. The geese arrive in mid-November and stay until early spring. They often congregate on sandbars, where they dine on small amounts of sand to help them digest their eelgrass meal. Other birds often spotted here include double-breasted cormorants, buffleheads, common loons, red-breasted mergansers, horned grebes, pigeon guillemots, and surf and white-winged scoters.

At 0.4 mile you'll arrive at a wood ramp that takes you across a marshy area filled with the fluffy brown plumes of cattails, arrow grass, pickerelweed, seaside plantain, beach pea, and cow parsnip. After 0.5 mile you'll arrive at the end of the trail and your turnaround point.

Miles and Directions

0.0 Start walking on the signed trailhead that begins on the left side of a chain-link fence on the far side of the parking area.

0.2 Pass a covered picnic shelter on the left.

0.4 Begin walking on a wood ramp that takes you through a marshy area.

0.5 Arrive at the end of the trail and your turnaround point. Retrace the same route back to your starting point.

1.0 Arrive back at the trailhead.

18 Mike Miller Educational Trail

This short interpretive trail explores a unique coastal forest ecosystem in the Mike Miller Educational Area. You'll hike past old-growth Sitka spruce trees and huge rhododendrons and over a small creek where you may see blue herons, ducks, and geese feeding.

Distance: 1.0 mile.
Approximate hiking time: 30 minutes to 1 hour.
Fees and permits: No fees or permits required.

Canine compatibility: Dogs permitted.
Maps: Maptech: Newport/Portland/Mount Hood/The Dalles, Oregon; USGS: Newport South, Oregon.

Finding the trailhead: From the junction of U.S. Highways 101 and 20, travel 2.8 miles south on US 101 and turn left (east) at the Mike Miller Educational Area sign. Continue on a gravel road for 0.2 mile to the signed trailhead on the left side of the road. *DeLorme: Oregon Atlas & Gazetteer:* Page 32, Inset 1, C1.

The Hike

This interpretive trail winds through a coastal forest made up of shore pine, Sitka spruce, Douglas fir, grand fir, and western hemlock. The route follows an old railroad grade that once was used to transport lumber (and later, passengers and mail) from Yachats to Yaquina Bay. Before you start the hike, be sure to pick up a trail brochure, which points out the trail's highlights.

The gravel trail is lined with Pacific rhododendrons that grow to more than 30 feet tall. This native plant has large,

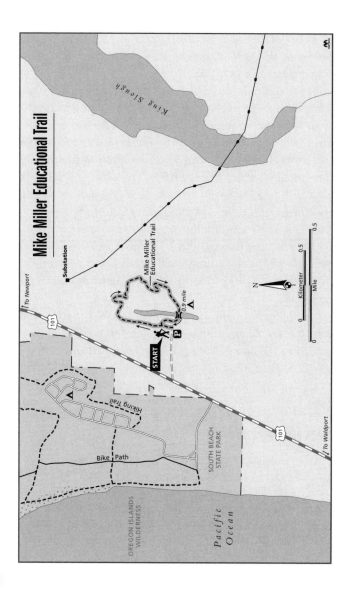

Mike Miller Educational Trail

Substation

Mike Miller
Educational Trail

0.9 mile

King Slough

To Newport

101

START

P

Hiking Trail

Bike Path

SOUTH BEACH
STATE PARK

OREGON ISLANDS
WILDERNESS

Pacific
Ocean

101

To Waldport

N

Kilometer   0.5

Mile   0.5

pink bell-shaped flowers that bloom in March and April. Although this is Washington's state flower, it does have a strong presence in Oregon.

After 0.2 mile the trail begins climbing, and the landscape changes from shore pine trees and rhododendron to large Sitka spruce trees. This noticeable difference is in part caused by the difference in soil types. The first section of the trail passes through a stabilized sand dune that once made up the shoreline of the Yaquina River. The sandy soil acts as a filter and does not retain water well. Hardy shore pine and rhododendron can tolerate this type of soil, but Sitka spruce trees require richer topsoil that retains more water.

As you hike through this large grove of trees, look for great horned owls roosting in the trees and listen for the owl's call, which is a series of hoots that can be three to eight notes long.

At 0.9 mile you'll cross a footbridge over a creek and wetland area. After crossing the bridge you have the option of turning left and walking down a short side trail to a viewing platform. Look for ducks, geese, and blue herons feeding in the creek, and listen for different melodies of resident frogs.

Miles and Directions

0.0 Pick up a trail brochure at the start of the hike. Walk 10 yards to a trail junction. Turn left and look for numbered signs that correspond to descriptions in the brochure.

0.9 Cross a footbridge over a creek. **Option:** After crossing the bridge, turn left and walk to a small viewing platform of the creek and marsh.

1.0 Arrive at a trail junction, ending the loop portion of the hike. Go left and walk 10 yards back to the trailhead.

19 South Beach State Park

This route offers plenty of opportunities to view wildlife and enjoy beach activities in South Beach State Park. You'll walk on the beach to the south jetty, where you can watch for wildlife and soak in the views of Yaquina Bay, Yaquina Bay Bridge, and the Yaquina Lighthouse.

Distance: 2.0 miles out and back (with longer options).
Approximate hiking time: 1 hour.
Permits and fees: No permits or fees required.

Canine compatibility: Leashed dogs permitted.
Maps: Maptech: Newport/Portland/Mount Hood/The Dalles, Oregon; USGS: Newport South, Oregon.

Finding the trailhead: From the junction of U.S. Highways 101 and 20 in Newport, travel 4 miles south on US 101 to the South Beach State Park turnoff. Turn right (west) and go 0.3 mile to a road junction. Turn left toward the day-use picnic area. Go 0.1 mile and turn left into a large parking area on the left. *DeLorme: Oregon Atlas & Gazetteer:* Page 32, Inset 1, D1.

The Hike

This beach hike, located in 434-acre South Beach State Park, features a large campground and many trails that wind through dunes, marsh, and the beach. You'll start this hike from the day-use area on a sandy trail that begins next to the rest rooms. The trail ascends a short sand dune and then descends to a long, flat sandy beach. Once you reach the beach, turn right (north) and enjoy the sounds of the crashing surf and salty coastal wind. As you walk north, look

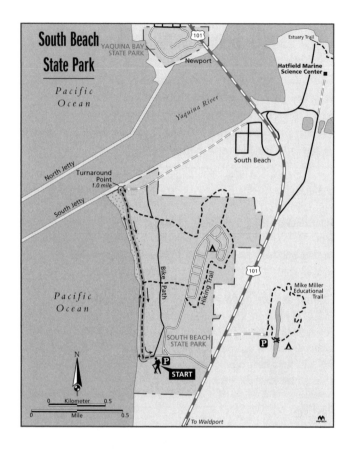

South Beach State Park

Pacific Ocean

YAQUINA BAY STATE PARK

Newport

101

Estuary Trail

Hatfield Marine Science Center

Yaquina River

South Beach

North Jetty

Turnaround Point
1.0 mile

South Jetty

Bike Path

Hiking Trail

101

Mike Miller Educational Trail

Pacific Ocean

SOUTH BEACH STATE PARK

START

N

0   Kilometer   0.5

0   Mile   0.5

To Waldport

offshore for brown pelicans flying above the waves, sandpipers running back and forth with the incoming tide, and
gulls resting in large groups on the beach.

After a mile of fun beach walking, you'll arrive at the
south jetty and the entrance to Yaquina Bay. From the south
jetty you may glimpse sea lions swimming in the channel
and a variety of ducks and other bird life. You'll also have

good views of the Yaquina Bay Lighthouse, boats traveling to and from Newport Harbor, and the graceful arch of the historic Yaquina Bay Bridge, which was completed in 1936.

From here you have the option of completing a loop back to your starting point. To complete the loop, turn right (east) on a doubletrack road and continue to the junction with a paved bike path. Turn right and follow the paved bike path for 1.2 miles back to your starting point.

While you are in this area, be sure to visit the Oregon Coast Aquarium (2820 Southeast Ferry Slip Road; 541–867–6846; www.aquarium.org). The aquarium contains several indoor and outdoor displays about Northwest plant and animal marine life. One of the most popular displays is the jellyfish tank—dozens of beautiful jellyfish swim freely in a circular tank in the middle of a large room filled with huge aquarium displays. Another favorite is the touch tank, where you can touch tidepool creatures such as starfish, sea anemones, starfish, and mollusks. The outside displays are just as fascinating. You can view California sea otters, harbor seals, and sea lions and walk through an outdoor aviary where you can watch tufted puffins, pigeon guillemots, common murres, and other seabirds swimming and feeding in a natural environment. Trails outside the aquarium lead through gardens of native plants with interpretive signs. The aquarium, which also has a bookstore and cafe, is open 10:00 A.M. to 5:00 P.M. daily mid-September through the end of May and 9:00 A.M. to 6:00 P.M. June through mid-September.

Miles and Directions

0.0 Start hiking on the sandy trail that starts next to the rest rooms. Arrive at the beach and turn right (north).

1.0 Arrive at the end of the beach at the south jetty (your turn-around point). **Option:** To complete the loop, turn right and continue on a doubletrack road to the junction with a paved bicycle path. Turn right onto the paved bicycle path and follow it for 1.2 miles back to your starting point.

2.0 Arrive back at the trailhead.

20 Seal Rock State Recreation Area

This route takes you on a short tour of rocky coastline and beach where you can explore tidepools and watch for abundant bird and marine life.

Distance: 0.4 mile out and back.
Approximate hiking time: 30 minutes to 1 hour.
Permits and fees: No permits or fees required.
Canine compatibility: Leashed dogs permitted.
Maps: Maptech: Newport/Portland/Mount Hood/The Dalles, Oregon; USGS: Waldport, Oregon.

Finding the trailhead: From the junction of U.S. Highways 101 and 20 in Newport, travel 14.4 miles south (or 5 miles north of Waldport) on US 101 to the Seal Rock State Recreation Area turnoff. Turn west and park in the day-use parking area. *DeLorme: Oregon Atlas & Gazetteer:* Page 32, Inset 2, A1.

The Hike

Seal Rock State Recreation Area covers five acres and features a beautiful coastal landscape made up of tidepools and rocky coastline. The basalt rocks and sea stacks present here are remnants of the Columbia River basalt flows that covered this area more than seventeen million years ago. The most dramatic rock formation in this area is Elephant Rock, which is part of the Oregon Islands National Wildlife Refuge. This important refuge comprises more than 1,400 islands, offshore reefs, and rocks that are located along the entire Oregon Coast and provides critical nesting grounds for more than 1.2 million birds as well as sea lions and seals.

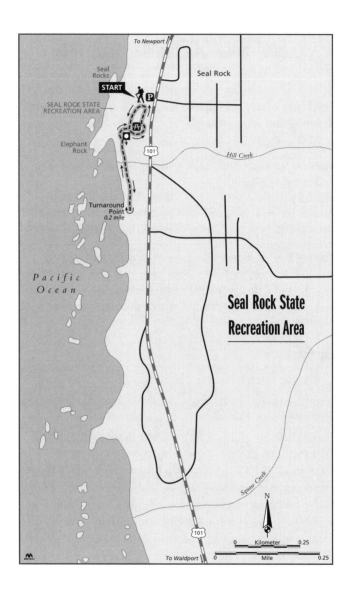

To Newport

Seal
Rocks

Seal Rock

START

SEAL ROCK STATE
RECREATION AREA

P

Elephant
Rock

101

Hill Creek

Turnaround
Point
0.2 mile

*Pacific
Ocean*

**Seal Rock State
Recreation Area**

Squaw Creek

N

0   0.25
Kilometer

0   0.25
Mile

101

To Waldport

Birds you may see here include pigeon guillimots, tufted puffins, common murres, pelagic cormorants, and western and glaucous-winged gulls.

Begin this hike by walking on the paved path on the left side of the rest rooms. Follow the path as it descends a pine-covered bluff to a wooden viewing platform with interpretive signs. After enjoying the gorgeous view of the rocky coastline, continue your descent on the paved path to the beach. Continue walking south on the beach, and be sure to explore the numerous tidepools at low tide.

The Alsea Indians hunted sea lions and their pups at this location and harvested clams and mussels from the rocky shore. These industrious people lived in about twenty small villages along the Alsea River and Alsea Bay. They lived in cedar-plank houses that housed up to four families. A large part of the tribe's diet was made up of salmon, sturgeon, flounder, and small game animals.

At the end of the beach, you'll reach your turnaround point. Retrace the same route back to the viewing platform, and then turn right and follow a paved path through a woodsy picnic area back to your starting point.

Miles and Directions

0.0   Start hiking on the paved path located on the left side of the rest rooms. Follow the path as it descends to a viewing platform with interpretive signs. After reading about the history and geology of the area, continue your descent.

0.1   Arrive at the end of the path and a long sandy beach. Walk south along the beach, and be sure to explore the tidepools that are accessible at low tide.

0.2 Arrive at the end of the beach (your turnaround point). Retrace the same route back to the viewing platform.

0.3 At the viewing platform turn right at the trail junction and follow the paved path through a picnic area back to the parking area.

0.4 Arrive back at the parking area.

21 Yachats 804 Trail

This short route, part of the Oregon Coast Trail system, takes you along a scenic section of rocky coastline in Yachats and then hits the beach, where you can enjoy the crashing surf and view abundant wildlife.

Distance: 3.0 miles out and back (with longer options).
Approximate hiking time: 30 minutes to 1 hour.
Permits and fees: No permits or fees required.

Canine compatibility: Leashed dogs permitted.
Maps: Maptech: Newport/Portland/Mount Hood/The Dalles, Oregon; USGS: Yachats, Oregon.

Finding the trailhead: From the bridge crossing the Yachats River in downtown Yachats, travel 1.1 miles north on U.S. Highway 101; turn left (west) onto Lemwick Lane toward the Smelt Sands State Wayside. Continue 0.2 mile to the road's end and a parking area. *DeLorme: Oregon Atlas & Gazetteer:* Page 32, Inset 2, B1.

The Hike

You'll enjoy the crashing waves and fresh sea breeze on this short, scenic trail located in the 3.9-acre Smelt Sands State Recreation Area, just north of the cozy community of Yachats (pronounced *Yah-hots*). The paved path parallels a stretch of rocky coastline that is made up of basalt, siltstone, and sandstone. This windblown trail is lined with salal, thimbleberry, and small Sitka spruce trees as well as less common ladies' tresses, golden-eyed grass, and leather grape fern. Scattered hotels are located just off the trail but do not cause too much of a distraction.

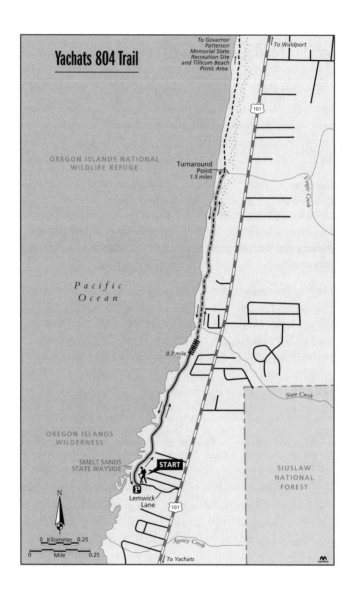

Yachats 804 Trail

To Governor
Patterson
Memorial State
Recreation Site
and Tillium Beach
Picnic Area

To Waldport

101

OREGON ISLANDS NATIONAL
WILDLIFE REFUGE

Turnaround
Point
1.5 miles

Vingie Creek

*Pacific
Ocean*

0.7 mile

Start Creek

OREGON ISLANDS
WILDERNESS

SMELT SANDS
STATE WAYSIDE

SIUSLAW
NATIONAL
FOREST

START

P

Lemwick
Lane

101

N

0   Kilometer   0.25

0   Mile   0.25

Agency Creek

To Yachats

This small section of coast was the center of a court battle for public ownership and right-of-way that started in the Lincoln County Circuit Court in 1984 and went all the way to the Oregon Supreme Court. Luckily the Oregon Supreme Court ruled in favor of allowing public access to this area in 1986.

As you hike on this route, you'll pass two spouting horns (areas where the ocean has pushed through cracks in the lava rock and sends sprays of water into the air) and small tidepools. After 0.7 mile you'll reach the end of the paved path. Walk down a set of stairs to the beach and continue 0.8 mile north to your turnaround point at Vingie Creek. From here you have the option of continuing 1.2 miles north to the Tillicum Beach picnic area. If you are looking for an all-day adventure, continue 4.8 miles north to the Governor Patterson Memorial State Recreation Site.

Miles and Directions

0.0   Start walking on the paved path as it parallels the edge of a rocky shoreline.

0.7   Arrive at steps leading to the beach. Walk down the stairs and continue north on the long sandy beach.

1.5   Arrive at Vingie Creek and a set of small sand dunes (your turnaround point). Retrace the same route back to your starting point. **Option:** Continue 1.2 miles north to the Tillicum Beach picnic area or 4.8 miles north to the Governor Patterson Memorial State Recreation Site.

3.0   Arrive back at the trailhead.

22 Cape Perpetua Trails

Take your pick of ten trails that wind through the 2,700-acre Cape Perpetua Scenic Area. Depending on the trail you select, you can experience a botanical wonderland of coastal forest, rocky tidepools, and other ocean spectacles, such as the geyserlike Spouting Horn and the narrow rock channel of Devil's Churn. Plan on spending a few hours at the Cape Perpetua Interpretive Center. The center provides a good introduction to the plants and animals that live here, as well as a look into the area's rich history.

Distance: Trails vary in length from 0.2 mile to 10.0 miles.
Approximate hiking time: 30 minutes to 3 hours, depending on the trail selected.
Permits and fees: $3.00 day-use permit. A permit can be purchased from the self-pay machine in the parking area or at the visitor center.
Canine compatibility: Leashed dogs permitted.
Maps: Maptech: Newport/Portland/Mount Hood/The Dalles, Oregon; USGS: Yachats, Oregon.

Finding the trailhead: From Yachats drive 3 miles south on U.S. Highway 101 to the Cape Perpetua Interpretive Center, located on the left (east) side of the highway.

From Florence drive 22.5 miles north on US 101 to the Cape Perpetua Interpretive Center, located on the right (east) side of the highway. *DeLorme: Oregon Atlas & Gazetteer:* Page 32, Inset 2, B2.

The Hike

If you're looking to explore the diversity of the Oregon Coast, you'll want to stop by the Cape Perpetua Scenic Area,

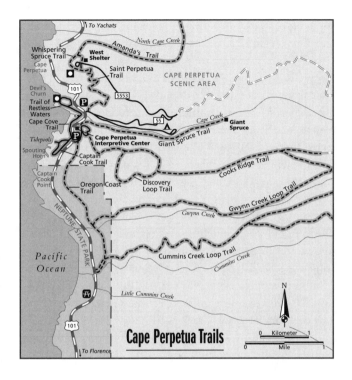

Cape Perpetua Trails

located 3 miles south of Yachats and approximately 22.5 miles north of Florence off US 101. This 2,700-acre area preserves large stands of coastal forest and rocky tidepools.

First, stop in and explore the interpretive center, where you'll receive a comprehensive overview of coastal ecology, tides and weather, whale migration, and the history of the Alsea Indian tribe. You'll also find interpretive exhibits, films, naturalist lectures, and a good selection of books about coastal ecology.

Each of the ten trails in the Cape Perpetua Scenic Area has something different to offer. For craggy tidepools, sealife, and a bit of Native American culture, hit the 0.6-mile Captain Cook Trail. The trail takes you past the historic Cape Creek Camp building, used by the Civilian Conservation Corp (CCC) from 1933 to 1942 to house the workers who built many of the park's trails and structures. The trail then dips under US 101 past an Indian-shell middens site—where Native Americans discarded shells from the mussels they collected for food. The trail ultimately leads you to rocky tidepools where you'll be able to view sea stars, mussels, hermit crabs, sea anemones, and purple sea urchins. Once you've finished exploring the tidepools, continue on to a viewpoint where you can watch for the geyserlike spray of Spouting Horn, an old sea cave with a small opening in its roof. Waves surge into this cave and shoot out of the small opening, creating a spectacular sea spray.

If you want to see a 500-year-old spruce tree, take the easy 2.0-mile (round-trip) walk on the Giant Spruce Trail. The trail parallels Cape Creek and leads you through an old-growth forest filled with ferns, salal, thimbleberry, and skunk cabbage. At the turnaround point is the trail's prize feature, an ancient Sitka spruce that's about 15 feet in diameter.

Another shorter trail that also gives you a feel for the diversity of the coastal forest is the 1.0-mile Discovery Loop Trail. If you love sweeping views, you'll want to hike the 2.6-mile round-trip Saint Perpetua Trail, which ascends the south side of Cape Perpetua on a series of fairly steep switchbacks and rewards you with excellent views (on a clear day) of Cape Foulweather to the north and Cape Blanco to the south.

For great views without the long hike, walk the easy, 0.25-mile Whispering Spruce Trail. This trail promises spectacular ocean views (on a clear day) and an opportunity to explore the West Shelter, a stone building built by the CCC.

If you're in for a longer hike, try the combination Cooks Ridge/Gwynn Creek Loop Trail. This 6.4-mile loop departs from the interpretive center and winds through old-growth forests, offering up several sneak peaks at the ocean. If you're interested in similar scenery but a lengthier hike, pack a lunch and strike out on the 10.0-mile Cummins Creek Loop Trail. From the interpretive center, the hike heads up the Cooks Ridge Trail and eventually hooks up with the Cummins Creek Trail for a return to the Oregon Coast Trail. Then it's straight back to the interpretive center.

If you love to watch the churning ocean, head down the 0.4-mile Trail of Restless Waters loop to the rocky tidepool known as Devil's Churn. The rough, porous texture of the shoreline rock here is evidence of its volcanic past. Roughly forty million years ago, offshore volcanoes deposited lava along the shoreline. As the molten rock cooled, hot gases within forced their way to the surface, creating the porous texture. The pounding surf carved into the rock to form a sea cave. At some point the roof of the cave collapsed, leaving behind the long, wide rock channel that forms Devil's Churn. The force of the waves crashing in the channel sends spectacular sprays of water dozens of feet into the air. If you're hiking with children or dogs, keep a close eye on them. The slippery surface of the rocks and sneaker waves can catch you off balance if you get too close to the edge of the channel.

Miles and Directions

The Whispering Spruce Trail is accessed 2.25 miles from the interpretive center via Forest Road 55 and then Forest Road

5553. The Saint Perpetua, Cape Cove, Giant Spruce, Captain Cook, Oregon Coast, Discovery Loop, Cooks Ridge/ Gwynn Creek Loop, and Cummins Creek Loop Trails can be accessed from the interpretive center. The Trail of Restless Waters starts from the Devil's Churn parking area, 0.7 mile north of the interpretive center off US 101.

A.   Whispering Spruce Trail—0.25-mile loop

B.   Saint Perpetua Trail—2.6 miles out and back

C.   Trail of Restless Waters—0.4-mile loop

D.   Cape Cove Trail—0.3 mile

E.   Giant Spruce Trail—2.0 miles out and back

F.   Captain Cook Trail—0.6-mile loop

G.   Oregon Coast Trail—2.6 miles out and back

H.   Discovery Loop Trail—1.0-mile loop

I.   Cooks Ridge/Gwynn Creek Loop Trail—6.4-mile loop

J.   Cummins Creek Loop Trail—10.0-mile loop

23 Heceta Head Lighthouse

Take a picturesque walk to one of Oregon's most pho-
tographed lighthouses. Nestled on the edge of the coastal
protrusion Heceta Head, the 205-foot-tall Heceta Head
Lighthouse is a welcoming beacon to ships and hikers alike.

Distance: 1.0 mile out and back.
Approximate hiking time: 30
minutes to 1 hour.
Permits and fees: $3.00 day-
use fee.

Canine compatibility: Leashed
dogs permitted.
Maps: Maptech: Newport/Port-
land/Mount Hood/The Dalles,
Oregon; USGS: Heceta Head,
Oregon.

Finding the trailhead: From Florence drive 12 miles north on U.S.
Highway 101 to the Heceta Head Lighthouse State Scenic Viewpoint
(also known as Devil's Elbow State Park) sign. Turn left (west) and
proceed 0.3 mile to the parking area. The hike begins on the north
end of the parking lot.

From Yachats drive 14 miles south on US 101 to the Heceta
Head Lighthouse State Scenic Viewpoint (also known as Devil's Elbow
State Park) sign. Turn right (west) and proceed 0.3 mile to the park-
ing area. The hike begins on the north end of the parking lot.
DeLorme: Oregon Atlas & Gazetteer: Page 32, Inset 2, C2.

The Hike

The Heceta (*huh-SEE-tuh*) Head Lighthouse stands as a
quiet sentinel on the Central Oregon Coast, shining its beacon 21 miles out to sea. This magnificent structure was built
in 1894 over a period of two years and at a cost of $80,000.
The stone was shipped to the site from Oregon City, and the

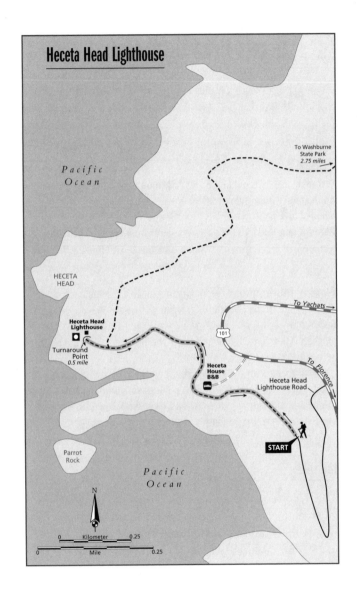

Heceta Head Lighthouse

Pacific Ocean

To Washburne
State Park
2.75 miles

HECETA
HEAD

Heceta Head
Lighthouse

Turnaround
Point
0.5 mile

To Yachats →

101

To Florence

Heceta House
B&B

Heceta Head
Lighthouse Road

Parrot
Rock

START

Pacific
Ocean

N

| 0 | | Kilometer | | 0.25 |
| 0 | | Mile | | 0.25 |

bricks and cement were brought in from San Francisco. Local sawmills supplied the wood, and the two-ton Fresnel lens was handcrafted and brought in by boat. The lighthouse and the scenic headland on which it sits owe their name to Captain Bruno Heceta, a Spanish captain who sailed his ship *Corvette* from Mexico to this part of the Oregon Coast. George Davidson, of the Coastal Survey, officially named the point in 1862.

The whitewashed lighthouse is accessed by a 1.0-mile out-and-back trail that starts at the north end of the Heceta Head Lighthouse State Scenic Viewpoint parking lot. The wide gravel path begins by climbing through a thick coastal cedar and fir forest dotted with sword fern, wild iris, and salal. Picnic tables have been set up so that visitors can enjoy the sweeping view of the rocky shore and rugged cape, as well as the 220-foot crowning arch of the Cape Creek Bridge. This bridge is just one of 162 bridges designed and built by Conde McCullough, head of the bridge division for the Oregon Department of Transportation from 1920 to 1935. In fact, McCullough designed virtually all the bridges on the Oregon Coast Highway, using innovative techniques to overcome the many challenges of building coastal bridges. One of the biggest challenges he faced was how to design bridges that used materials other than steel, which doesn't hold up well in the stormy, salty air of the Oregon Coast. He also needed a material that was strong enough to span the region's wide estuaries. His solution was to use the Freyssinet method, developed in France, to build bridges that used arches made of prestressed concrete. Construction on this scenic highway began in 1927, and by 1936 the final bridges were finished.

At Mile 0.2 you pass the immaculately maintained light keeper's house. Built in 1893, this lovely Queen Anne–style house is now being used by the USDA Forest Service as an interpretive center and B&B. In spring you may spot the teardrop-shaped petals of white lilies scattered along this section of trail. A white picket fence surrounds the house, which has three upper-story rooms. Picture windows offer a grand view of the rocky coast and lighthouse, and everything is topped off with a bright red roof.

Continue another 0.3 mile to reach the lighthouse and your turnaround point. Just before you reach the lighthouse you have the option to turn right and hike 3.0 miles north to Washburne State Park. After you've soaked in the views of the lighthouse, glance to the offshore promontory called Parrot Rock, an important nesting area for the Brandt's cormorants. Tours of the lighthouse are offered daily and include climbs to the top, where the intricate Fresnel lens is on display.

Miles and Directions

0.0 Start at the north end of the parking area. Before you begin, check out the interpretive signs that provide an in-depth view of the history of the lighthouse and light keeper's residence.

0.2 Pass the light keeper's house on your right. Just before the lighthouse you'll arrive at a trail junction. Continue straight. **Option:** Turn right and hike north. You'll arrive at Washburne State Park in 3.0 miles.

0.5 Reach 205-foot Heceta Head Lighthouse, your turnaround point.

1.0 Arrive back at the parking area.

About the Author

Lizann Dunegan is a freelance writer and photographer who specializes in writing about outdoor activities and travel. She has been hiking trails in the Northwest for more than ten years and is often accompanied by her partner, Ken Skeen, and her two border collies, Levi and Sage. Lizann is the author of several books about the Northwest, including *Canine Oregon, Hiking Oregon, Hiking the Oregon Coast, Trail Running Oregon, Mountain Biking Northwest Oregon, Road Biking Oregon, Best Easy Day Hikes Portland, Best Easy Day Hikes Bend and Central Oregon,* and *Insiders' Guide to the Oregon Coast.* An avid mountain biker, cross-country skier, sea kayaker, violinist, and cellist, she lives in Portland, Oregon.

FALCON GUIDES®

From nature exploration to extreme adventure, FalconGuides lead you there. With more than 400 titles available, there is a guide for every outdoor activity and topic, including essential outdoor skills, field identification, trails, trips, and the best places to go in each state and region. Written by experts, each guidebook features detailed descriptions, maps, and advice that can enhance every outdoor experience.

You can count on FalconGuides to lead you to your favorite outdoor activities wherever you live or travel.

BEST EASY DAY HIKES

The Best Easy Day Hikes series is designed for the hiker who wants to explore the backcountry but doesn't have time for a lengthy or difficult hike. These books are compact, easy-to-use guides to accessible and scenic trails across America.

4 ¼" x 7" · paperback · maps